Food from the *Heartland*

Glenn Andrews

Food from the HEARTLAND

The Cooking of America's Midwest

PRENTICE
HALL
PRESS

NEW YORK • LONDON • TORONTO • SYDNEY • TOKYO • SINGAPORE

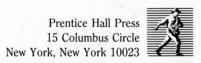

Prentice Hall Press
15 Columbus Circle
New York, New York 10023

Copyright © 1991 by Glenn Ellis Andrews

Library of Congress Cataloging-in-Publication Data

Andrews, Glenn
Food from the heartland : the cooking of America's Midwest / Glenn Andrews.
p. cm.
Includes index.
ISBN 0-13-323254-9
1. Cookery, American—Midwestern style. I. Title.
TX715.A56669   1991 641.5977—dc20   89-8847
CIP

Designed by Carla Weise/Levavi & Levavi

Manufactured in the United States of America

10 9 8 7 6 5 4 3 2 1

First Edition

Contents

Dedicated with love to my children, Kate, Bob and Candace, all of whom have helped me in innumerable ways in the writing of this book (and otherwise!).

And to Craig, Kim and Sean, my children-in-law.

To Meghan, my lovely granddaughter, who's becoming a good cook at a very early age.

To Julie Fallowfield, my agent, but more importantly, my friend.

To my wonderful editor, Toula Polygalaktos, who was a joy to work with.

And with thanks to all the generous Midwesterners, mentioned throughout the book, who gave me their time and their recipes.

Introduction

These are the foods of my childhood, of happy, lazy carefree days in the Midwest, the heartland of America. When I eat these foods, I feel I'm coming home.

It's been a long time since I actually lived full time in the Midwest. When I was quite young, my parents moved East, to the New York area. It was in the middle of the Depression, and my father was in search of fame and fortune—or at least enough of the latter with which to support us.

Eastern life came as a shock. Everything seemed different, but especially the food most people ate. At first, my mother still cooked the good old foods which I felt were the only proper things to eat: German potato salad, wilted lettuce, spareribs with sauerkraut, fried green tomatoes with cream gravy and such. Then, as my father prospered, to these were added some trendy Eastern foods which just didn't seem right at all.

Fortunately, though, moving East didn't totally end my childhood connections with the Midwest and its food. We visited relatives and friends in Illinois and Missouri with some regularity and I spent most of every summer and quite a few Christmases with my maternal grandparents in Mount Pleasant, a small town in southeastern Iowa.

These were joyous visits. There's a real warmth to Midwestern people, an outpouring of love and of giving. They reach out their arms and hold you close. They're strong—physically, morally and spiritually. They give you a heartwarming feeling of family and security and of being loved.

Midwesterners work hard, as a matter of course, but they also relax thoroughly, gregariously and happily. Those Midwestern trips of mine were full of laughter and parties. Breakfast "coffees," luncheons, afternoon gatherings, bridge parties, dinner parties, evening occasions of various sorts, covered-dish or potluck suppers and marvelous picnics which sometimes lasted all day. Food was a thing to be shared. To invite someone to a meal was to show warmth and friendship. To give someone a cherished recipe was to give a present of great worth.

So it's no wonder that Midwestern people have such a tremendous interest in food. Unless you've lived there, you can't imagine how much of their time is spent thinking and talking about recipes and various ways of cooking.

And it's not just Midwestern women who have this strong interest in food, either. The men may not talk about recipes as much as the women, but they are often the ones who know the most about where to obtain the very best ingredients. My grandfather, for instance, would make sure that on our trips to Des Moines, the state capital, we'd come back by way of Amana, one of the earliest American cooperative communities, to pick up some of the magnificent home-cured hams and bacon produced there. He was also the one who took us to Pella, Iowa, a Dutch settlement, for their wonderful cookies and sent to Newton, Iowa, for the most superb blue cheese, produced there by a member of the Maytag washer and dryer family.

My grandfather knew exactly where to go for the finest steaks and he had sources for quail and other game. He even brought home a piece of buffalo meat one day. My grandmother gulped a bit, but after giving the matter some brief but careful thought, she cooked the buffalo as she would have any regular pot roast. (And that's what it tasted like, too—any regular pot roast.)

When I married and settled down in a one-room Manhattan apartment, my grandfather must have worried about how and what I was going to eat. At any rate, he sent me food packages, encased in dry ice and sent by airmail, on a regular basis. Gorgeous corn-fed steaks often, and once in a while a whole boxful of tiny quail. Sometimes he sent some of the beautiful Maytag blue cheese, and once he sent a whole Amana ham. It was exciting for me to be able to invite my New York friends over to sample some *real* food.

Roadside stands were irresistible to my grandfather. His specialty was melons, particularly watermelons and canteloupes, or as he called them, muskmelons. He taught me how to tell if canteloupes were worth buying by looking at the webbing on their shells and seeing if their smell was right and how to "thump" watermelons to see if they were properly ripe—and also how to get the watermelon vendor to "plug" a melon, or cut a small piece out of it so we could actually taste a bit before we bought.

I don't recall his ever buying corn on the cob or other vegetables or fruits. It wasn't because my grandparents raised their own. Although my grandfather owned a farm with what I've been told was the most productive soil in Iowa, he and my grandmother didn't live there. They lived in town, and my grandmother grew flowers, not vegetables. (My grandfather rented his land to a farmer, and the only condition he imposed was that gypsies be allowed to camp there. That's one of the reasons I loved him so much.)

The main reason my grandparents didn't buy much in the way of fruits and vegetables was that astonishing amounts of them arrived at the back door every day, all summer long. My grandfather, you see, was a doctor, and many of his patients, lacking money, paid him in produce they'd grown themselves or with dairy products, eggs or the specialties of their kitchens.

We were given soft green lettuce, ripe and glorious tomatoes, incredibly thick cream, fertile eggs, jams, jellies, pickles, sauerkraut and, once in a while, jars of home-canned chicken, with white meat swimming in a yellow, deeply delicious broth.

One summer, my grandfather must have done major surgery on every member of a large family of strawberry growers, because strawberries were left outside the kitchen door every morning for weeks. We had them for every meal—plain, with ice cream, *in* ice cream, in frozen salads, in fruit cups, in strawberry shortcake, in cakes and pies and pancakes and in every way my grand-mother's imaginative brain could conceive. Can you imagine ever saying, "Oh, no, not strawberries again?" We finally did. It was actually a relief when strawberry season came to an end.

We could, in fact, distinguish the seasons by the offerings we'd find outside the kitchen door, and we certainly ate primarily seasonal food. I remember the first peas of those early Iowa summers—no other peas come close to their flavor. From the middle of summer on, we received tomatoes fresh from the vine and never chilled (let alone gassed, as is done to so many commercial tomatoes); they were bliss. Corn on the cob meant mid- to late summer and was delivered late in the day so there'd be only an hour or two between the picking and the cooking and eating. That's the way to live!

Most of the dishes I grew up thinking of as "Midwestern" come from farmhouses and are basically the dishes cooked by the early settlers and their descendants. The majority of these settlers were themselves descended from people from Great Britain and continental Europe who landed on and lived in the East Coast of America in the seventeenth and eighteenth centuries. Many of them began to move West early in the nineteenth century because, if you can believe it, they felt the East was becoming too crowded.

By the last quarter of the nineteenth century, then, the American Midwest was well populated with families who had come there from New England, New York, all the Middle Atlantic states, Virginia and the Carolinas. These families, originally English,

Scottish, Dutch, German, Welsh, Irish (I happen to carry the blood of all these myself), Swedish, Norwegian, etc., became neighbors and began to exchange recipes. They intermarried, too, and their traditions and their foods became gloriously intermingled.

Then came added glamour. Some of the French came down from Canada, and from Europe came an astonishing array of people, cultures and foods—Czech, Swiss, Polish, Romanian, Russian, Hungarian, Italian and so on. These people have caught and added to the Midwestern spirit of warmth and strength and love—and how their foods have enriched us! Most of the recipes in this book are from the old-time, early settler families, but there are also a large number of samples of the newer, exciting ways of cooking which have come into the area recently—in the last one hundred or so years, that is.

All these foods seem to me to represent old-fashioned virtues, ones that Midwestern people don't have to "return" to because they've never left them. The foods are as honest, unpretentious and heartwarming as the people.

It's also true that these foods spare the pocketbook. It isn't just that Midwesterners don't use truffles or pâté de foie gras in their everyday cooking (and believe me, they don't). The main thing is that hardly anything is wasted. Leftover mashed potatoes become mashed potato patties and even chocolate cakes. Miscellaneous bits and pieces of vegetables go into soups and stews. Leftover chicken turns up with noodles or in casseroles or salads. Leftover meats become crisp hashes or creamy salads. The fat that cooks off so many things (sausage, bacon, goose, duck, whatever) turns up frying the morning's ham or the dinner's potatoes—and adding greatly to the flavor.

It's routine in the cooking of the Midwest for one chicken to serve twelve or more people. I don't know of any other peoples, except possibly the Chinese, as adept at making a little bit of meat or poultry go a long way.

It's hard to pin down the geographic boundaries of the Midwest (or Middle West, as it is also known). Certainly the entire states of Ohio, Indiana, Michigan, Wisconsin, Illinois, Minnesota, Iowa and Missouri are included. To these, we can add all or part of North and South Dakota, Kansas and Nebraska. Now extend our wobbly line down to include at least the northern parts of Arkansas, Kentucky and Oklahoma. This, roughly, is the Midwest.

Within this book, you'll find recipes from all these states as well as recipes from all the large ethnic groups and most of the smaller ones. You'll find, among many other fabulous foods, Limpa, the Swedish rye bread, aromatic with orange peel and fennel. German Potato Salad, hot and strongly flavored with bacon, onion and vinegar. *Chodnik*, a cold Polish soup with the cooling flavors of cucumbers, beets, dill and sour cream. Veal Paprika, its smooth sour cream sauce contrasting with fine noodles tossed with poppy seeds and buttered almonds. Fried green tomatoes, crisp and fruitlike, served with peppery cream gravy. Leaf lettuce served with nothing but a touch of Lemon-Cream Dressing. Snap Doodle, a coffee cake studded with pools of melted brown sugar, nuts and cinnamon. Buttermilk pie, subtle and cheesecakelike, in a crust enlivened with the taste of oranges. Pickled Peaches, spicy and mouth-watering.

How I love this food! Nowadays, in contrast to the little girl I used to be who was shocked by the trendy foods of the East Coast, I cook and delight in the cuisines of India, Indonesia, Mexico, all of Europe and various provinces of China. I've come a long way, but home to me is still the Midwest, and real food will always mean the foods of home. I can't manage to get to the Midwest very often these days, but simply by cooking its wonderful dishes, I can get the feeling I crave of coming home.

A Note to the Reader

In a world newly committed to spare eating and low-cholesterol food, I almost feel a bit guilty telling you how to cook the fine foods of the Midwest, laden as they are with butter, cream, sour cream, lard, bacon fat, cheese, and eggs.

This, though, is the way the people of the heartland have been cooking and eating for generations, and somehow most of them have stayed thin and lived to very respectable ages. (My Aunt Camilla, who's from Missouri, says it's because they've always worked so hard, and she's probably right.)

However, they do sell a lot of margarine in the Midwest, so feel free to use it if you want. (Or combine a pound of real butter with ⅔ cup salad oil and a tablespoon of lecithin granules dissolved in a very little warm water and use that, instead.) Similarly, you could use "imitation" sour cream. I'm not saying you *should*, but you *could*. Or follow a long-standing Midwestern custom and use white vegetable shortening of the Crisco variety instead of butter in the dessert recipes.

Lard was and is a staple in the kitchens of the heartland. It makes the tenderest and flakiest pie crust you could imagine and adds flavor to many dishes, but you could substitute margarine for this, too. Bacon fat is used in dish after dish. Every drop of it is saved when bacon is cooked and it's considered a treasure. Not only does it fit right in with the Midwestern ideas of frugality but it also adds considerable flavor. Sausage fat, too, fills both these requirements, and goose fat is perhaps the most cherished of all. Here, though, you could substitute salad oil for any of the fats. My own solution, when I become overcome by guilt at the amount of cholesterol I'm consuming, is to use half bacon or sausage or goose fat and half salad oil.

Black pepper is called for in many recipes. In any other sort of cookbook, I would exhort you to grind it freshly from a pepper mill. This is not a Midwestern concept, though. These great cooks have almost always used store-bought ground pepper, and in their recipes it seems just fine.

Vanilla is another matter. Real, pure vanilla is essential to the success of many of the dessert recipes. Artificial vanilla or "vanillin" just doesn't taste the same at all. I, and many others with a heartland heritage, find it highly unpleasant.

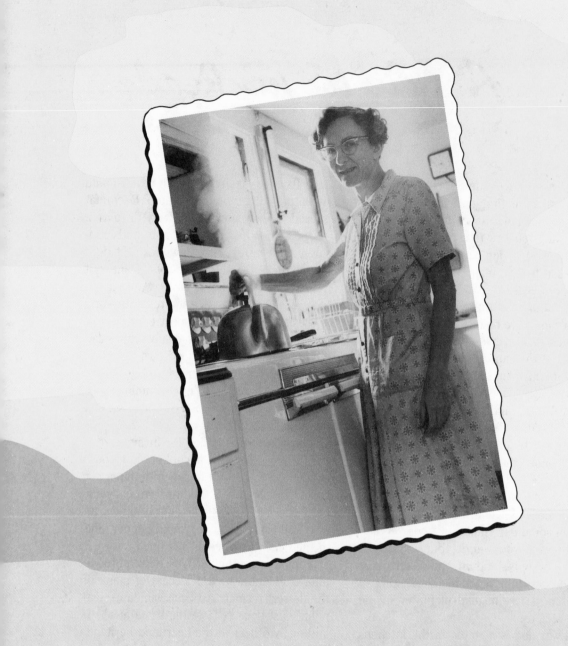

Soups

N othing demonstrates the basic, inherent qualities in both Midwestern people and their foods better than their soups. They, both soups and people, are unpretentious and delightful. Good soups, good people.

Many of these soups are based on either chicken or beef broth. If you wish, you can use canned broths or even granules or bouillon cubes, but for true, full flavor, your own, homemade broths will be best. You'll find instructions for these within the recipes for Boiled Chicken on page 51 and Midwestern Boiled Beef on page 24.

North Dakota Beer-Cheese Soup

Beer and cheese go well together, and never more so than in this excellent soup. It's very warming—just the thing for those long, cold Dakota winters.

1/4 cup minced onion or scallion
2 tablespoons minced carrot
1/4 cup minced green pepper
3 tablespoons butter
2 tablespoons flour
3 1/2 cups chicken broth (see page 51)
8 ounces cheese (Cheddar or Swiss), grated
1 1/2 cups beer (stale beer is fine)
Salt and pepper to taste

Sauté the onion, carrot and green pepper gently in the butter for 5 minutes. Stir in the flour and cook, stirring, for 2 or 3 minutes, then add the chicken broth. Stir well. Simmer for 5 minutes, then add the cheese and beer. Heat slowly, stirring often and whisking if necessary, until the cheese is completely melted. Add salt and pepper if needed. • *SERVES 4.*

Some Dakotans insist on dark beer in their beer-cheese soup, but a light beer, especially a European one, will do, too.

Midwestern Corn Chowder

If you'll look at this recipe closely (or better yet, try it), you'll see that it is exactly like New England–style clam chowder except that corn has been substituted for the clams. It's fun to think of the pioneers setting out from New England's rocky hillsides for what must have seemed a paradise of flat, rock-free, easy-to-till land—and adapting the recipes from home to the ingredients in their new world.

1/4 pound salt pork, rind removed, cut in small dice
2 medium onions, minced
3 medium potatoes, peeled and diced
1/2 cup water
3 cups corn, cut from the cob (or frozen or canned)
3 cups milk
Salt and pepper to taste

Cook the salt pork in a saucepan over medium heat until it begins to brown. Add the onions and cook, stirring often, until they, too, begin to take on color. Then add the potatoes and water and simmer, covered, until the potatoes are tender, about 10 minutes. Add the corn and simmer for 5 minutes more. Stir in the milk and season to taste. Heat very slowly, stirring often.
• *SERVES 4 to 6.*

Barley Soup

Barley Soup is straight from the old country—any number of old countries. You'll find it, or close approximations of it, in Austria, Germany, France, Great Britain and all over the American Midwest. Without being heavy, this is a very satisfying, heartwarming soup.

1 medium onion
1 small carrot
1 stalk celery
2 tablespoons butter
1/2 cup pearled barley
5 cups chicken broth (see page 51)
1/2 cup heavy cream
Salt and pepper to taste

Mince the onion, carrot and celery, but not too finely. Cook them in the butter with the barley for 5 minutes over medium heat, stirring, then add the chicken broth. Cover and simmer until the barley is tender, about 1 to 1½ hours, depending on the size of the barley. Just before serving, stir in the cream and season to taste with salt and pepper.
• *SERVES 4 to 6.*

Old-Time Tomato Soup

Not so very long ago, it was a common practice in the Midwest to preserve the beautiful tomatoes of summer by canning them not only by themselves but also in the form of a concentrated soup base. When you wanted tomato soup in the winter, you would heat the soup base in one pot and an equal amount of milk in another, then combine them. (This procedure prevented curdling.) Here is a recipe of that sort, but cut down to manageable, one-meal size—the old recipes call for tomatoes by the bushel.

2 cups peeled, seeded and chopped tomatoes
2 tablespoons minced onion
2 tablespoons minced celery
2 tablespoons minced green pepper
1 tablespoon butter
1 bay leaf
1 clove
½ teaspoon baking soda
2 cups rich milk (or make part of it light cream)
Salt and pepper to taste

Cook the tomatoes, onion, celery, green pepper, butter, bay leaf and clove together over medium-low heat for 25 minutes. Add the baking soda and remove the bay leaf and clove.

When you're ready to eat, heat the milk to just under the boiling point in a separate pan, then stir it into the hot tomato mixture. Season with salt and pepper.
• *SERVES 4.*

Hospital Soup

The idea behind hospital soup, according to the people of Hungarian descent in Indiana who swear by it, is that if you drink it, you'll get well—no matter what your problem is. I make no medical claims for it. What matters is that it's remarkably tasty, and it does seem to cheer you up!

4 tablespoons butter
2 tablespoons caraway seeds
3 tablespoons flour
4 cups water or beef broth (see page 24)

In a saucepan, cook the butter over low heat until it just begins to brown. Add the caraway seeds and flour and continue to cook very slowly, stirring, until the flour browns and you hear little popping sounds from the seeds. Now add the water or broth all at once. Stir well and simmer for 15 minutes. Taste the soup now to see if it needs salt—it might if you use water, which is more traditional than broth in this soup.

Strain the seeds out if you wish.
• *SERVES 4.*

Ukrainian Sauerkraut Soup

This recipe, of Ukrainian origin, is from Mrs. Wasyl Kilik, mother of my friend Stephanie Smith. Mrs. Kilik cooked it to the delight of all for most of her ninety-six years. There are yellow split peas in here as well as sauerkraut; nevertheless, the name remains sauerkraut soup. Mrs. Kilik always at least doubled this recipe because it was eaten in quantity by her many children, grandchildren and great-grandchildren, but the amount given here is enough for smaller groups.

- ½ cup less than 1 pound yellow split peas, rinsed
- 6 cups water
- ½ cup finely minced salt pork
- 1 cup chopped onion
- 2 tablespoons flour (Mrs. Kilik browned the flour lightly in the oven before using)
- 2 pounds sauerkraut, lightly rinsed and drained

First, cook the split peas. Cover them with the water, bring to a boil, then turn down the heat and simmer, covered, for 3 or 4 hours, or until very soft, almost mushy. Add more water if needed.

Now brown the salt pork and onion. Stir in the flour and cook, stirring, for 3 or 4 minutes, then add about 1 cup of liquid from the split peas and simmer for 10 minutes. Add this mixture along with the sauerkraut to the split peas, and simmer for 15 minutes more. • SERVES 6 to 8.

Pioneer Cabbage Soup

Pioneer Cabbage Soup goes back to the days when the pioneers had fresh meat and vegetables only in the late spring, summer and early fall—except for meat and vegetables that were cured or dried or could survive, at least for a while, in "cold cellars." Necessity being the mother of invention, these restrictions created great soups such as this one.

- 1 smoked ham hock
- 2 quarts water
- 2 cups chopped cabbage
- 1 onion, chopped
- 2 carrots, chopped
- 1 cup peeled and chopped turnips
- ¼ pound smoked sausage (optional)
- ¼ teaspoon dried herbs (basil, oregano or marjoram)
- ½ cup dried pea beans or other dried beans, soaked and cooked until tender
- Salt and pepper to taste (none may be needed)

Simmer the ham hock in the water in a large kettle, covered, for 1 hour. Add the cabbage, onion, carrots, turnips and sausage and simmer, still covered, for another hour, or until everything is very tender. Now remove the ham hock and sausage, add the herbs and beans and continue to simmer for 20 minutes more. Remove the skin from both ham hock and sausage, cut the meat into small pieces and return to the soup. Season with salt and pepper.
• SERVES 6.

Wisconsin Borscht

Borscht, one of the great soups of the world, came to the Midwest, and especially Wisconsin, with the Russian immigrants. It fit right in, as did they, though it changed a bit as it traveled. For instance, kvass, a fermented drink made from black bread and an important ingredient in old-country borscht, was replaced by lemon juice, vinegar or citric acid (sour salt).

What distinguishes borscht from the other cabbage soups of the heartland is the addition of beets, which give it its characteristic red color. Dill's important, too, as is a topping of sour cream.

This is hot borscht, the most popular kind. Some people, and especially those of Ukrainian heritage, add enough meat to make it definitely a full-meal soup. There's a cold version, too, which is made primarily of beets and does not commonly contain cabbage.

1 cup chopped onion
1 ½ cups chopped beets
½ cup thinly sliced carrots
3 cups beef broth (see page 24)
1 cup tomato purée
1 cup diced potatoes
1 ½ cups shredded cabbage
1 tablespoon lemon juice or mild vinegar or 1 crystal citric acid (sour salt, available in grocery stores)
Salt and pepper to taste
Sour cream for garnish
Fresh dill or dried dill weed for garnish

Cook the onions, beets and carrots gently in the beef broth for 15 minutes. Add the tomato purée, potatoes and cabbage and simmer for another 15 minutes. Stir in the lemon juice, vinegar or citric acid and season with salt and pepper. Serve each bowlful topped first with a spoonful of sour cream, then with a sprinkling of dill.
• *SERVES 6 to 8.*

Ohio Potato Soup with Egg

This unusual potato soup contains not only eggs but also cubes of bread. It's extremely warming and filling and could easily pass for dinner—or at least supper—when served with a salad.

2 cups peeled, diced potatoes
½ cup minced celery
3 cups water
3 cups milk
2 cups bread cubes
3 eggs
1 tablespoon butter
Salt and pepper to taste

Boil the potatoes and celery in the water until soft but not dissolved. Add the milk and heat carefully, not letting it scorch, then stir in the bread cubes. Now add the eggs one by one, stirring briskly after each addition. Add the butter, then season with salt and pepper. • *SERVES 6.*

Lowlands Carrot Soup

The idea for carrot soup is usually credited to the settlers from the lowlands of Holland, Belgium and Flanders, but those from any country could have worked it out (and, in fact, probably did) all by themselves. The color is bright and the taste is delightful.

8 medium-size carrots, thinly sliced
1 large onion, thinly sliced
1 large potato, peeled and thinly sliced
4 tablespoons butter
1 quart chicken broth (see page 51)
½ teaspoon sugar
2 cups rich milk
Salt and pepper to taste

Cook the carrots, onion and potato slices in the butter over very low heat for about 15 minutes, stirring often. The vegetables should not brown at all.

Add the chicken broth and sugar and simmer, covered, for about 20 minutes, or until the vegetables are very soft. Run through a blender, food processor or food mill, then return to the pot and add the milk. Reheat gently and season with salt and pepper.
• *SERVES 4 to 6.*

Fresh Lima Bean Soup

As far as I know, there's no such thing as a single-vegetable soup in Midwestern cookery, but this one comes close. There's a bit of onion for flavor (who could make a vegetable-based soup without onion?), but the effect is pure, though glorified, lima bean.

1 pound shelled lima beans (or 1 10-ounce package frozen)
1 medium onion, chopped
2 tablespoons butter
4 cups chicken broth (see page 51)
Salt and pepper to taste

Cook the lima beans and onions very slowly in the butter for 5 minutes. Add the chicken broth and simmer the soup until the limas are very soft. (The time varies with the size of the beans and whether they are frozen or not.)

Run through a food processor, blender or food mill, then return to the pot, reheat and season with salt and pepper.
• *SERVES 4 to 6.*

Baked Bean Soup

This is one bean soup which can be made without hours of preliminary soaking and/ or simmering, simply because the bulk of that sort of work was done in the original making of the baked bean dish on which it is based. It turns up in the heartland wherever baked beans are cooked, and that's just about everywhere.

I suspect that the pureeing of the soup is done in an attempt to hide its leftover origin. The name, though, comes right out and gives the show away: Baked Bean Soup is its forthright title—and it's a fine, forthright soup, too.

2 cups leftover baked beans
1 medium onion, chopped
4 cups water
1 cup cooked or canned tomatoes (optional—many prefer not to use them)
1½ tablespoons butter
1½ tablespoons flour
Salt and pepper to taste

Simmer the beans and onions in the water in a stockpot for 30 minutes. Add the tomatoes if you wish to use them, then run the mixture through a blender, food processor or food mill. Return to the stockpot.

Melt the butter in a small pan. Add the flour and stir over medium heat for 3 or 4 minutes. Add a ladleful of the baked bean puree and stir well, then mix into the stockpot. Season with salt and pepper.
• *SERVES 4 to 6.*

Sausage-Ball Soup

There are many other sausage soups in the Midwest, most of them filled with such things as macaroni, celery, carrots and so on—all the contents of the home kitchen. This simple Wisconsin version, though, is probably the best of them all—and definitely the quickest.

1 cup chopped onion
5 cups beef broth (see page 24)
½ pound sausage meat
3 cups potatoes, peeled and diced
Salt and pepper to taste

Add the onion to the broth in a medium-size saucepan and bring to a boil. Shape the sausage meat into small balls and drop carefully into the broth. Turn down the heat; cover and simmer for 1 hour. Add the potatoes and cook for about 20 minutes, or until they are tender, adding more water if necessary. Season with salt and pepper.
• *SERVES 4 to 6.*

Velvet Soup

Most Midwestern soups are hearty and of the stick-to-the-ribs variety. Not Velvet Soup. It's delicate and soft and just right for a light first course. (Some people add bread crumbs to it, though. This addition makes it a bit more sturdy and textured—more of a Velveteen Soup. Others add shreds of cooked chicken.)

The very simplest Velvet Soup is made by adding milk or cream to an equal amount of heated chicken broth (see page 51). Heat to just under the boiling point, stirring constantly.

FOR FANCIER, MORE VELVETY VELVET SOUP

1 quart chicken broth (see page 51)
2 tablespoons cornstarch
2 tablespoons water
1 cup light cream
4 egg yolks, beaten
Salt and pepper to taste
Whipped cream for serving

Combine the chicken broth with a mixture of the cornstarch and water and cook, stirring, until slightly thickened. Add the cream and bring almost to a boil over medium heat, then pour slowly over the egg yolks, stirring continuously and vigorously.

Now reheat the soup very gently. Some cooks transfer it to a double boiler at this point. Others just use low heat and extreme caution. Taste for seasoning.

Pass a bowl of whipped cream at the table when you serve the soup. Some may want it, others won't. • *SERVES 4 to 6.*

Emergency Mashed Potato Soup

This is an emergency well worth having. Many Midwestern cooks prepare extra mashed potatoes whenever they're having them just so they can have this soup the next day.

As is true with many "emergency" dishes, there can't be a formal recipe for this soup. It's just a matter of fiddling around with what you have. Here's the general pattern:

Cook a little minced onion gently in some butter until it's soft. Stir in leftover mashed potatoes and add chicken broth and perhaps a little milk or light cream until the soup reaches the consistency you want. Heat gently. Taste to see if salt and pepper are needed.

Blue Satin Soup

Blue Satin Soup is an example of the newer, more sophisticated ways of cooking in the heartland. It was created by Mrs. Donn Campbell, wife of the president of Maytag Dairy Farms in Newton, Iowa, from recipes sent in by several of their blue cheese customers. It's a lovely soup.

Maytag cheese is dear to my heart, since my grandfather used to send me packages of it with some regularity—and because I do believe it's the best blue cheese ever. The company was founded in 1941 by two members of the Maytag appliance family. The Maytag Company makes its cheese by hand from the milk of its own Guernsey herd. It's aged in special caves and is generally a fine example of the Midwestern joy in exceptional food.

4 tablespoons butter
¼ cup finely minced onion
¼ cup finely minced green pepper
¼ cup finely minced celery
½ cup flour
2 cups chicken broth
4 ounces blue cheese (preferably Maytag, of course)
1 cup light cream
1 cup milk
Black pepper to taste
2 ounces dry sherry (optional)
Chives, croutons or sour cream to garnish (optional)

Melt the butter in a medium-size saucepan and cook the minced vegetables in it slowly, until soft but not brown. Add the flour and cook, stirring, for 3 to 4 minutes, then stir in the chicken broth and simmer for about 2 minutes. Add the blue cheese, crumbled, and stir until it has melted, then add the cream and milk and heat gently to serving temperature. Add the black pepper and, if you wish, the sherry. (The soup's just as good, if not better, without it.) Garnish to your taste. • *SERVES 4.*

Balkan Bread Soup

Immigrants from the Balkans and Central Europe brought with them the idea for this simple but satisfying soup. For the hardworking homesteaders, a hungry but not always prosperous group, the ingredients were always on hand.

½ cup finely chopped onion
2 tablespoons any sort of fat
6 cups beef broth (or water, if times were really hard)
6 slices bread, preferably whole wheat, crumbled
4 eggs
1¼ cups light cream
Salt and pepper to taste

Cook the onion in the fat over medium heat in a saucepan until wilted but not brown. Add the broth and the bread and simmer for 15 minutes. Now beat the eggs with the cream. Stir in a few spoonfuls of the hot broth, then, working very quickly, stir the egg mixture into the saucepan. Season with salt and pepper. • *SERVES 4 to 6.*

Fisherman's Catch Soup

Most of the fish brought home by Midwestern anglers is turned into main dishes, but sometimes, especially when a lot of fish has been brought into the kitchen recently, the cook's mood runs more toward soup. Whatever the sort of freshwater fish, large or small, it can go into this piquant concoction.

You won't find many recipes in this book which call for wine, but some Midwesterners have used it in their cooking for generations. It's even made in various spots—Missouri, Illinois and Iowa, for instance. Those who don't use it simply substitute a little lemon juice and get the same general effect.

¾ cup diced onion
2 tablespoons butter or salad oil
2 to 3 pounds trout, pike, bass or other freshwater fish, cleaned— whole if small, cut into pieces if larger
½ pound tomatoes, coarsely chopped
2 quarts water
1 cup cooked rice
½ cup white wine or the juice of 1 lemon
Salt and pepper to taste

Cook the onion in the butter or oil over medium heat in a large saucepan for a few minutes, until well wilted but not brown. Add the fish, tomatoes and water and simmer for 20 minutes. Now stir in the cooked rice and wine or lemon juice, season to taste and reheat the soup. • *SERVES 4 to 6.*

Dutch Pea Soup

If you go to Pella, Iowa, to the Strawtown Inn, in a restored building of authentic Dutch decor, you can order this specialty of Eunice Kuyper, the owner. (You'll find more about Pella, a place of happy memories for me, on page x.)

Mrs. Kuyper has been generous enough to share her recipe with me. I'm giving you the recipe exactly as it came from her. This is a woman who teaches cooking as well as running an inn and obviously knows her way around a recipe.

Don't plan on eating much else when Dutch Pea Soup is on hand. A freshly made hot bread—biscuits or corn bread, for instance—will be all you need.

1 pound whole or split peas
2 pounds fresh pork hocks or
  country-style ribs
3 quarts water
1½ cups celery, cut fine, with tops
3 medium onions, chopped fine
3 potatoes, diced
½ cup chopped parsley
Salt and pepper to taste
4 smoked sausages or hot dogs,
  sliced

Soak the peas in 1 quart water overnight. Drain. Add 1 quart cold water and the meat and cook over low heat for about 2 hours, skimming the foam for the first 5 minutes, then covering and stirring occasionally.

Add the next 5 ingredients and cook over low heat for 1 hour. Add the sliced sausages or hot dogs 15 minutes before serving.
• *SERVES 6 to 8.*

Ham Bone–Split Pea Soup

As I've said elsewhere, nothing goes to waste in a Midwestern kitchen. Ham bones in particular are coveted, used primarily in such soups as split pea. If there's no ham bone available, a smoked ham hock can be substituted. Also, if a ham has been boiled, the "liquor" can be saved—frozen, in fact—and used at a later date for the water in soups of this sort.

To make the sort of traditional ham bone–split pea soup found all over the Midwest, follow the recipe above for Dutch Pea Soup, substituting a ham bone for the fresh pork, adding ¾ cup minced carrot and a bay leaf and omitting the potatoes.

White Bean Soup or Senate Soup

This is the soup served in the United States Senate dining room. So how does that make it Midwestern? Well, in 1907, Senator Knute Nelson of Minnesota, a powerful man who chaired the Senate Committee on Rules, decreed that this bean soup must be served every day in the Senate dining room. (Later, Joe Cannon, a despot in the House of Representatives, issued a similar order there, which was modified by Congressman Bob Traxler of Michigan to state that the soup must be made only with Michigan white—navy—beans.)

The only difference between the Senate and House soups is the worthwhile addition of chopped, browned onion in the Senate version. I have seen recipes called "Senate Bean Soup" which not only include mashed potato but state that this is a very important element in the soup.

True, that makes a nice soup, too, but it's gilding a fine Midwestern lily. Senator Nelson would not have approved.

1½ pounds small white navy or pea beans
2 quarts hot water
¾ pound smoked ham hocks
1 large onion, chopped
2 tablespoons butter
Salt and pepper to taste

Wash and pick over the beans, then "run them through hot water until they are white again." (I know that sounds strange, but those are the directions given out at the Senate. Furthermore, they work—and it will make more sense after you try this system.)

Put the beans in a large pot with the 2 quarts of hot water and ham hocks. Simmer until the beans are tender, which may be in about 2½ hours or may take longer, depending on your beans. Cook the onion in the butter and add to the soup. Add the salt and pepper at serving time.
• *SERVES 8.*

Black Bean Soup

Some Midwesterners serve their black bean soup with chopped hard-boiled egg on top. Others prefer a slice of lemon for garnish and a bit of flavor. Still others use both. I'm of the lemon-slice school myself, and follow the example of an old family friend who always added some lemon juice, too.

2 cups black "turtle" beans
2 quarts water
¼ cup chopped onion
¼ cup chopped celery
2 tablespoons butter
Salt and pepper to taste
1 tablespoon lemon juice
Chopped hard-boiled egg and/or thinly sliced lemon for garnish (optional)

Put the beans in a large pot with enough cold water to cover by about 1 inch. Bring to a boil and cook for 3 minutes, then remove from the heat and allow to soak for 1 hour. Drain.

Cook the onion and celery over medium heat in the butter just until limp, then add the soaked, drained beans and 2 quarts of fresh cold water. Simmer until the beans are very soft, 3 to 4 hours, adding more water if needed. Now run the soup through a food mill or puree it in a food processor or blender. Reheat and season with salt and pepper. Stir in the lemon juice just before you're ready to serve it. Garnish, if you wish, with the chopped egg and/or lemon slices. • *SERVES 8.*

Mrs. Martin's Lentil Soup

When the days begin to shorten and the air begins to chill, it's lentil soup season. Some lentil soups are made with a ham bone or ham hock (of course), but many prefer a lighter and less strongly flavored soup such as this.

1 pound lentils, washed but not soaked
2 quarts beef broth (see page 24)
2 celery stalks, minced
2 medium onions, minced
1 bay leaf
Salt and pepper
1½ tablespoons white or cider vinegar
4 frankfurters, precooked and thinly sliced, for garnish (optional)

Simmer the lentils, broth, celery, onions and bay leaf, covered, for about 1½ hours, or until very tender. Remove the bay leaf and season with a little salt and pepper and the vinegar.

The thinly sliced frankfurters are placed on top of each serving. They're optional, but they do make the soup a favorite with children. • *SERVES 6 to 8.*

Polish Dill Pickle Soup

The name "Pickle Soup" may be startling, but the soup is wonderful. Those of Polish extraction claim mysterious medicinal powers for dill pickle soup, especially when ingested by pregnant women. All I know is that it has a pleasant, piquant taste—I didn't know about it when I was having my three children, though I can easily imagine developing "cravings" for it. Poles often cook spareribs or other pieces of pork with the soup, then remove them before serving, but most other people prefer this simpler version.

    7 cups chicken broth (see page 51)
    1 large potato, peeled and finely
        diced
    1 small carrot, minced
    2 medium-size dill pickles, minced
        or coarsely grated
    ½ cup sour cream
    1 tablespoon flour
    1 tablespoon lemon juice
    Salt and pepper to taste
    Juice from the dill pickle jar
        (optional—see below)

Cook 3 cups of the chicken broth and the potatoes together over medium heat for 20 minutes, or until the potatoes are very tender. Run through in a blender or food processor, then return to the pot. Add the rest of the chicken broth, the pickles and the carrot and simmer together for another 20 minutes.

Now combine the sour cream and flour in a bowl and quickly stir in 1 cup of the hot broth mixture. Stir this into the soup and simmer gently for 3 to 4 minutes. Add the lemon juice and season with salt and pepper. If you should want the soup to be more sour, add a little juice from the pickle jar.
• *SERVES 6 to 8.*

Winter Fruit Soup

Many of the fruits of summer such as cherries are always canned ("put up") for the winter. But a tradition still persists of using dried fruits to make a soup designed for winter use. My mother used to astonish and delight Easterners by serving it as a first course at dinner parties. She served it hot, but some others chill it, even though it's cold outside. (And still others serve it, hot or cold, for dessert or breakfast. This is a multipurpose dish.)

1 package mixed dried fruit
   (approximately 11 ounces)
3 cups water
2 tablespoons fresh lemon juice
¼ cup sugar
½ cinnamon stick
1 teaspoon grated orange or
   lemon rind
Whipped cream or sour cream for
   garnish

Soak the dried fruit, following the directions on the package, then cook it over medium-low heat with the water, lemon juice, sugar, cinnamon stick and orange or lemon rind until very tender.

Remove the cinnamon stick and check to make sure there are no prune pits in the soup. Serve hot, with each bowl topped with a spoonful of whipped or sour cream.
• *SERVES 4.*

Chlodnik

In Poland, its home country, a number of such different ingredients as shrimp or chopped, cooked veal turn up in Chlodnik, *a cold yogurt-based soup. In our heartland, though, there are many versions of this refreshing soup, most of them simplified. Some contain beets, some don't, and the same can be said for chopped hard-boiled eggs, cucumbers and onions. In an occasional* Chlodnik, *the yogurt has been replaced with (choose one) sauerkraut juice, dill pickles and their juice, buttermilk, sour cream or a combination of sour cream and beer. The shrimp are there only in the fancier city-folk versions. It's just another example of Midwestern independent thinking.*

1 cup beets, cooked and cut into
   julienne strips (cheat and use
   canned beets, if necessary)
1 large cucumber, peeled, seeded
   and diced
1 fairly small dill pickle, minced
¼ cup minced scallions
¼ cup minced radishes
½ cup chicken broth (see page 51)
1 quart yogurt
2 tablespoons minced fresh dill or
   1 tablespoon dry dill weed

Combine all the ingredients and chill well.
• *SERVES 4 to 6.*

Cold Cherry Soup

If a restaurant on the East or West coasts of the United States were to offer a cold fruit soup (and they sometimes do), they would no doubt be considered innovative and daring, but cold soups made from various fruits are commonplace in many parts of the Midwest. The concept came to the area with the Scandinavian settlers and also with those from Czechoslovakia, Germany, Hungary and Rumania. Cherry soup seems to be the most appreciated, and no wonder, since it's mouthwateringly good. In Europe, the soup is usually made with wine, but most Midwesterners prefer lemon juice.

This is a summer recipe. For the cold-weather version, see the next recipe, Winter Fruit Soup.

4 cups tart cherries, pitted
1 cinnamon stick, broken in half
1 whole clove
1 lemon, thinly sliced (divided)
Water (see below for amounts)
1/3 cup sugar
2 tablespoons fresh lemon juice
2 tablespoons cornstarch
Sour cream (optional—see below)

Cook the cherries, cinnamon stick, whole clove and half the lemon slices in 1 cup water in a medium-size saucepan over medium heat until the cherries are soft, about 15 minutes. (Reserve the remaining slices of lemon.) Put through a food mill or strainer, discarding the cinnamon stick, clove, etc. Measure the resulting liquid, add enough water to make 1 quart and return to the saucepan.

Add the sugar and cook and stir until it is dissolved. Stir in the lemon juice. Now combine the cornstarch with 1/4 cup of water. Add this to the soup in the saucepan and stir continuously over medium heat until thickened.

Chill well. Serve with one of the reserved lemon slices on top of each bowl. (Or, following a Hungarian tradition, top each serving with a spoonful of sour cream.)
• *SERVES 4.*

Meat

The meat in the middle of the country is superb, and so are the regional ways of cooking it. Here, more than perhaps anywhere else, the Midwesterner's true delight in food shows up.

The secret to the high quality of the meat is that it's from animals fed the fabled corn of the area. The cornfields which stretch for mile after mile in perfect checkerboard patterns are primarily this "feed" or "field" corn, not "sweet" corn for the table (although there's a good bit of that, too). It's feed corn that's meant when Iowans stand and sing, "Ioway, Ioway, that's where the tall corn grows!" or when farmers, worrying about the progress of their crops, insist that corn should be "knee high by the Fourth of July."

Flank Steak Pinwheels

Flank steak has some interesting attributes. Midwesterners—of course, canny cooks that they are—take advantage of these. For one thing, if you broil flank steak and slice it thinly on an extreme slant, it is the original London broil, tender and very flavorful. For another, flank is usually much less expensive than sirloin, rib, tenderloin or the other steak cuts. The attribute which shows most clearly in this recipe is that this cut is so versatile in character that it can be stuffed, rolled, tied and made into fascinating dishes.

1¼ pounds flank steak
Salt and pepper
4 slices bacon
1½ tablespoons lard or other fat
2 tablespoons water

Sprinkle the steak with salt and pepper, then lay the bacon on top of the meat. Roll up and tie with string in 4 places. Cut into 4 sections, each enclosing a bacon slice. Lay these flat and sear them in the hot fat in a frying pan with a lid until browned, then add the water. Cover and simmer for about an hour, turning once. • *SERVES 4.*

There is one other cut of beef that makes nice pinwheels—skirt steak. However, since it's the cut of choice for the currently fashionable fajitas, it's become rather expensive.

Beef Pot-Dinner

Picture a big farmhouse kitchen in, say, Nebraska. The rest of the family and the hired hands are out working in the fields. The apron-clad mother has been working in the kitchen for hours, canning vegetables and making pies. Finally she realizes that the time to eat is growing near, so she brushes the flour off her hands and quickly puts together a Beef Pot-Dinner which she can serve with just one vegetable side dish—Buttered Green Peas with Mint (page 109), for instance. When the field-workers return, everything's ready, the kitchen smells wonderful and big smiles come across their faces as they stamp their feet on the doormat and come into the house.

This lovely cliché of a scene doesn't occur too often these days. The father's apt to be running some of his immense farm machinery alone. The children are doing their homework on their computers. The mother is rushing home from her job as vice-president of the local bank. Still, Beef Pot-Dinners endure, and no wonder, since they're quick and so good. They still make the kitchen smell inviting and still bring smiles to the faces of all.

½ pound bacon
1½ pounds beef chuck or round, cut into thin strips
3 large onions, thinly sliced
4 potatoes, peeled and thinly sliced
Salt and pepper
Water

Cut the bacon slices in half and use them to line the bottom and partway up the sides of a Dutch oven or other large, heavy pot with a lid. Put in the strips of beef, then the onions, then the potatoes. Sprinkle on a little salt and pepper. Cook over moderately high heat for about 3 minutes, then slowly pour in enough water to come up to the level of the onions. Now turn down the heat, cover the pot and cook for 45 minutes, or until the beef is tender and the water has evaporated. (Alternately, cook in a 325° F oven.) If there's any water left in the pot, boil it off quickly over medium heat. • *SERVES 4.*

This is just my own preference, but I think Beef Pot-Dinner is at its best when the bacon on the bottom of the pot is *almost* burned.

Chicken-fried Steak

Chicken-fried Steak is old-fashioned, but it still turns up on many dinner tables and on the menus of innumerable little restaurants in the heartland. It's considered the very best thing you can do with round steak, a cut which needs tenderizing.

1½ pounds round steak, cut ½ inch thick
½ cup flour
Salt and pepper
¼ cup bacon fat, lard or other fat
½ cup water
½ cup milk or light cream

Mix the flour with a little salt and pepper and pound it well into both sides of the meat with the edge of a heavy plate or a special meat mallet, if you happen to have one. When the meat has become considerably thinner, and thus somewhat tenderized, cut it into 4 serving-size pieces.

Heat whatever fat you're using in a large frying pan and cook the pieces of steak in it until browned. Now turn down the heat, pour off most of the fat and add the water and milk or cream, stirring and scraping up any brown bits on the bottom of the pan. Cover and simmer until the steak is fork-tender. • *SERVES 4.*

Rib Roast of Beef with Yorkshire Pudding

The English influence in Midwestern cooking shows up most brilliantly in this classic dish. Traveling Midwesterners who order it at Simpson's in the Strand in London find it tastes of home—although they've probably never seen a joint of beef anything like the size of those served routinely in Britain.

In England, the Yorkshire pudding is usually cooked under the roast. Some clever Midwesterner worked out this version, which is simpler and tastes just the same.

1 6-pound rib roast (the first 3 ribs from a standing roast)
1 teaspoon salt
¼ teaspoon black pepper
Popover batter (see page 148)

Rub the beef with the salt and pepper. Place it, fat side up, in a shallow roasting pan (you don't need to use a rack). Bake at 500° F for 20 minutes, then turn the heat down to 350° F and roast for an hour longer, or until the interior of the meat has reached 125° F on a meat thermometer, at which point it will be medium-rare in the middle and more well done on the outside. Remove the meat from the oven and place on a heated platter. Turn the oven heat to 400° F.

Now put about ¼ inch of the hot fat which has melted off the roast into a 10 × 10-inch pan. (Add butter or other fat if you

don't have enough from the roast.) Heat the pan and its fat briefly in the oven, then pour in the popover batter. Bake until beautifully puffed and brown, roughly half an hour.
• *SERVES 6 or more.*

If you want gravy: The juices which come out when you carve the meat are a fine sauce just as is, but most Midwesterners prefer a real gravy. To make it, leave about 4 tablespoons of fat in the roasting pan. To this, add 3 tablespoons flour. Cook and stir over medium-low heat for a few minutes, browning the flour very lightly, then add 2½ cups of beef broth or water. Stir, scraping the bottom of the pan to get up all the little browned bits which will add to the flavor. When the gravy thickens a bit and comes to a boil, add salt and pepper to taste. Strain if you wish—most people don't bother.

Grandma's Waistline

This recipe comes from a very nice book, Bach for More, *published by the Junior Committee to benefit the Cleveland (Ohio) Orchestra. (It's a sequel to their first book,* Bach's Lunch. *If you don't get the jokes, say the titles aloud.) My thanks to the committee for permission to give you the recipe—I wouldn't want you to miss this one. The title "Grandma's Waistline" is fun. The recipe creates a wondrous dish.*

1 tablespoon sugar
2 large onions, thickly sliced
1 pound white navy (pea) beans
2 tablespoons suet, chopped
1 2½-pound chuck roast (or other cut suitable for pot roasting), cut into 2-inch-wide strips
6 medium potatoes, peeled and cut in half
Salt and pepper to taste

Place the sugar in a heavy kettle. Heat until it browns, only a few seconds. Cover with a thick layer of onion rings. In a separate pan, bring the beans to the boiling point and rinse under cold water; place over the onions and sprinkle with the suet; top with the meat, and then with the potatoes. Season with salt and pepper and add water to cover. Cook over very low heat, covered, for 12 hours, adding water as needed to keep it moist. Turn off the heat before going to sleep; turn it on the next morning for another 12 hours, adding water as needed. When the potatoes are brown, it is ready to serve. The longer it cooks, the better it is. Mix gently before serving. • *SERVES 8 or more.*

When I made this amazing recipe, I did it following the instructions above and using a Dutch oven, but you could probably make it more easily if you use a Crockpot. As you see, it takes about thirty-six hours to make a proper Grandma's Waistline, including the overnight sitting time, but there's very little actual work involved.

Midwestern Boiled Beef

Midwestern Boiled Beef is not drastically unlike the boiled beef of any given European country, except that it's almost always served with the vegetables that are cooked in it. Then the various Midwestern groups add their own touches. In Minnesota, for instance, rutabagas are often used in addition to the usual vegetables, and a little ginger is added to enliven the taste. In Wisconsin, some people serve it with two sauces, both based on a sour cream–enriched white sauce—one with added horseradish, the other with dill.

This is a very basic boiled beef. It gives you a splendid dinner plus meat for sandwiches, salads and hash, and it also creates the perfect beef broth to use in soups. Brisket of beef is the cut of choice, but short or cross ribs or shin work well here, too.

3 pounds "boiling" beef (see above)
6 small onions, peeled but left whole
2 whole cloves
1 bay leaf
1 large stalk celery, cut into 6 pieces
2 teaspoons salt
½ teaspoon black pepper
Cold water to cover
6 medium-size carrots, scraped
6 small purple-top turnips, scraped
6 medium-size boiling potatoes, not peeled

Put the beef, onions, cloves, bay leaf, celery and salt and pepper in a large kettle or Dutch oven. Add cold water to cover. Bring to a boil and keep it boiling for 3 to 4 minutes while you take off the scum which will form. Now turn the heat down, cover the kettle and simmer for 2½ hours, or until tender. Add the carrots, turnips and potatoes and cook for another ½ hour, or until they're tender, too. (Alternately, cook your boiled beef in a Crockpot.)

You can serve the beef on a platter, surrounded by the vegetables. Better yet, though, you can serve the sliced beef along with the vegetables in individual soup plates or bowls, moistened with broth and with a cup of broth on the side for each person to drink or add to the bowl. Horseradish is traditional with boiled beef, and pickles go well with it, too. • *SERVES 8 or more.*

OPTIONAL ADDITIONS
Leeks, trimmed and added with the carrots, turnips and potatoes.

Rutabagas, peeled and thickly sliced, added with the carrots, turnips and potatoes. (In Minnesota, they tend to remove the rutabagas at the end, mash them and return them to the kettle to thicken the broth. I wouldn't think of doing this, since I always have further plans for the broth.)

Cabbage, cut in chunks and cooked separately, lets its strong flavor overwhelm the broth.

Jerky

Beef jerky is a popular treat which can be bought in many kinds of stores (I've even seen it for sale in gas stations), but it started out as a clever Native American way to preserve buffalo meat or venison.

Oklahoma has representatives of more Native American tribes—at least sixty-five of them—than any other state, mainly because of the government-mandated forced march known as the Trail of Tears which moved such tribes as the Seminoles, Creeks, Chickasaws, Choctaws and Cherokees here from the South in the early part of the nineteenth century.

Originally, jerky was made over campfires, but today the home oven with the help of "liquid smoke" produces the woodsy flavor. The marinade is a modern touch, designed both to flavor and to tenderize. Today, even some Native Americans use such things as teriyaki sauce to marinate the meat, but the seasonings below are more typical.

1 ½ pounds lean top round steak, trimmed of all gristle and fat
¾ cup water
1 large clove garlic, minced (or use 1 teaspoon garlic powder)
½ teaspoon ground black pepper
1 teaspoon chili powder
½ teaspoon Wright's Natural Hickory Seasoning ("liquid smoke"), available in most markets

Partially freeze the meat to make for easy slicing, then cut across the grain into strips about ⅛ to ¼ inch thick. Combine the remaining ingredients, add the meat and marinate for at least 3 or 4 hours, but preferably overnight.

Now lay the strips directly on an oven rack, placed at least 2 inches above a pan to catch the drippings. (Alternate method: Place a toothpick in one end of each strip and hang them from the oven rack over a pan.) Bake at 200° F for 4 to 6 hours, or until dry enough to crack but not break when bent.
• *YIELD: 1½ pounds fresh beef becomes ¾ pound jerky, which will keep indefinitely at room temperature if tightly sealed.*

Sauerbraten with Gingersnap Gravy

Here is my mother's recipe for this sensational dish, which is just one example of the German influence on Midwestern cooking. Her recipe called for an extra cup of water plus ¼ cup flour for thickening. I don't find these necessary. Don't leave out the gingersnaps, though—they're very important to the flavor.

    4 to 5 pounds boiling beef—chuck,
        round or rump
    3 tablespoons salt
    2 cups cider vinegar
    1 cup water (plus 1 more cup—
        optional, see below)
    4 whole cloves
    2 bay leaves
    6 peppercorns
    2 tablespoons shortening or salad
        oil
    1½ cups sliced onion
    ¾ cup sliced carrot
    ½ cup sliced celery
    ¼ cup brown sugar
    ¼ cup flour (optional—see below)
    10 crushed gingersnaps

Place the meat in a large bowl or strong plastic bag and sprinkle it with the salt. Combine the vinegar, 1 cup of water and the spices and bring to a boil. Let cool slightly, then pour over the meat. Seal well and refrigerate for 2 or 3 days, turning the meat occasionally.

Now remove the meat from the marinade and dry it well with paper towels. Brown it in a large Dutch oven or other covered pot in the shortening or salad oil. Add the vegetables and sprinkle on the brown sugar. Strain the marinade and add 1 cup of it to the pot. Cover and cook slowly on top of the stove for 3 hours.

Remove the meat, strain the liquid and skim off the fat.

Now, if you wish, combine the second cup of water with the flour. Add this combination to the gravy in the pot and cook and stir until thickened. I skip this step.

Add the crushed gingersnaps to the gravy and cook for a few minutes more.
• *SERVES 8 to 10.*

Scandinavian Beef Stew

The real name of this stew is Lobscouse, and it was originally made by Scandinavian sailors who were far out at sea and had little in the shipboard larder. The sailors just took the few ingredients they had on hand, threw them in a pot with a little water and a fine dish was born.

Back on shore, the sailors showed others how to make it. Some of them came to the New World, settled in places like Minnesota and Wisconsin and carried on the tradition. Their neighbors, after one taste or even one whiff of the glorious aroma of lobscouse, started making it, too, and the name became Scandinavian Beef Stew. My family and I think it's the best stew, and one of the most soothing foods, in the world.

2 pounds stewing beef, cut in
   1-inch cubes
½ pound salt pork, cut in ½-inch
   cubes
Water to cover
4 medium potatoes, peeled and
   cut into chunks
2 medium onions, peeled and cut
   into chunks
Salt and pepper to taste (just a little
   salt)

Put the beef and salt pork in a large saucepan and cover with water. Bring to a boil, then turn down the heat and simmer, uncovered, for about 1½ hours, or until the beef is tender.

Now add the potatoes and onions and a bit of salt and pepper. Simmer for 25 minutes more, or until the potatoes begin to fall apart, checking every 5 minutes or so to make sure there's enough water. If, on the other hand, the stew is too liquid when it's finished, cook it down quickly over medium heat. • *SERVES 4 to 6.*

Beef à la Lindstrom

You'll find this tangy, remarkable Swedish version of the hamburger patty in Minnesota and Wisconsin. It's still cooked in Sweden itself, too. I can't tell you who or what Lindstrom was or is, but I do know that there are only two famous Midwestern dishes with "à la" in their names: Beef à la Lindstrom and pie à la mode.

1 pound ground beef
1 small onion, finely minced
1 large potato, peeled, cut into small dice, boiled and drained
⅓ cup minced Pickled Beets (see page 196)
2 egg yolks
1 tablespoon rinsed and chopped capers
2 tablespoons light cream or rich milk
Salt and pepper to taste
1 tablespoon butter and 1 tablespoon salad oil

Combine everything except the butter and salad oil. Let the mixture sit, refrigerated, for at least an hour. Form into 4 fat cakes. Cook in the hot butter and oil until crisp and brown on both sides. • *SERVES 4.*

Braised Short Ribs, Iowa Style

Short ribs cooked this way were my grandfather's favorite food. If you were to order them in a restaurant, the water in the recipe might well be replaced by wine, but this would never have happened in my grandparents' house, since Patchie, my grandfather, was adamantly against liquor in any form. (I've been told he single-handedly kept Henry County, Iowa, "dry" for several decades after the end of Prohibition.)

Notice the chili powder in this recipe. The closest most Midwesterners have come to "Tex-Mex" food is chili con carne, but a small amount of chili powder is common in many dishes with a tomato-based sauce. It adds just the right amount of zip.

2 pounds meaty short ribs of beef, cut into 2-inch pieces
2 tablespoons flour
2 tablespoons lard, bacon fat or salad oil
1 large onion, sliced
1 cup tomato puree or sauce
½ cup water
½ teaspoon chili powder
Salt and pepper to taste

Dredge the short ribs lightly with the flour and brown them on all sides in the lard, bacon fat or oil. Pour off all but about 1 tablespoon of the fat, then add the onion. Cook and stir briefly, then add the rest of the ingredients. Simmer, covered, turning the ribs twice, for 1½ to 2 hours, or until tender. Serve with mashed potatoes or noodles. • *SERVES 4.*

Mary Ann's Beef Patties

This is the way my father's mother, Mary Ann Ellis, used to cook chopped meat patties when she was raising her seven children in Kansas City, Missouri, around the end of the nineteenth century. With that many mouths to feed, the meat-stretching qualities of these patties must have come in handy, but more than that, her children, or at least my father, thought they were marvelous.

1 pound chopped beef
¼ cup chopped onion
4 slices bread, crumbled
1 egg
Salt and pepper
Milk to moisten
2 tablespoons butter, bacon fat, or any other fat

Combine the beef, onion, bread, egg, salt and pepper with enough milk to make a moist but firm mixture. Let sit for at least 10 minutes, then shape gently into patties.

Cook in medium-hot fat until both sides are well browned.
• *MAKES 6 to 8 medium-size patties.*

Swedish Meatballs

"Swedish Meatballs" seems to be a generic term in the Midwest, applied to absolutely any meatball recipe. Of all the "Swedish" meatballs I've encountered, these are by far my favorites. They're also the most like those made in Sweden, though I suspect the touch of ginger may have been added in this country by a clever heartlander.

1 pound lean ground beef
¼ teaspoon ground ginger
1 teaspoon salt
⅛ teaspoon black pepper
1½ cups beef broth, divided (see page 24)
2 tablespoons butter
¼ cup light or heavy cream (optional)

Combine the beef, ginger, salt and pepper with just enough beef broth (perhaps ¼ cup) to make the mixture hold together. Shape into small balls. Brown in a frying pan in the butter, then add the rest of the broth and simmer, covered, for 15 minutes. Now, if you wish, add the cream and cook briefly. Serve with mashed potatoes, rice or noodles. • *SERVES 4.*

Cincinnati Chili

No one can give you THE recipe for Cincinnati Chili, the spicy treat devoured by the thousands of bowlfuls every day in various Cincinnati chili parlors. On a trip there, I tried to pry the secret out of the people who run the Skyline chain. They laughed at me. My friend Jane Heimlich, because she wrote a column for the Cincinnati Enquirer, *was able to visit the newspaper's files and make copies of several versions. Friends of hers gave me still other variations. The one point on which everyone agrees is that it's a Greek-inspired way with an American (not truly Mexican, mind you) delight. At any rate, it certainly is inspired.*

Here's my version, a product of much experimentation, combining other people's ideas and adding my own. To me, it tastes exactly like the chili I was in search of. It may not resemble any chili you've ever tasted (except in Cincinnati), but it's delicious. Skyline and the other chains serve their chili on spaghetti, with or without added toppings of chopped raw onion, beans and grated American cheese. The list of ingredients is long, but I feel that each one is necessary to achieve the true Cincinnati taste.

1 1/2 pounds ground lean beef (chuck, for instance)
1 1/2 cups chopped onion
1 teaspoon butter or salad oil
1 cup chopped tomatoes (canned are fine)
6 ounces tomato paste
1 quart water
3 tablespoons chili powder
3/4 teaspoon cinnamon
2 teaspoons sugar
1 tablespoon vinegar
1 teaspoon Tabasco sauce
1/2 teaspoon ground cumin
1/2 teaspoon marjoram
1 bay leaf
1/2 teaspoon ground coriander
1/2 teaspoon salt
1/2 teaspoon cocoa powder

Brown the ground meat and onions in the butter, then run them together through a meat grinder or in a food processor. Put into a large saucepan with all the other ingredients and simmer, covered, for 1 1/2 hours, stirring occasionally, Remove the bay leaf and serve the chili plain, in bowls, or with spaghetti and/or the onions, beans and cheese mentioned above.

• *SERVES 6 to 8.*

Veal Paprika with Poppy Seed Noodles

This marvelous recipe has come down through four generations of my family. It has an obvious Hungarian origin (though I don't), but all I know is that everyone I have ever served it to has loved it. I once multiplied everything by 60 and, with much help, served it to 360 people at a community luncheon. It was a big hit; I have never been the same.

2 pounds boneless veal, cut in
  1-inch cubes
Salt and pepper
1 clove garlic, peeled
2 tablespoons olive or other salad
  oil
1½ cups water
¾ cup sour cream
1 teaspoon paprika

FOR THE NOODLES

6 ounces very fine noodles
3 ounces coarsely chopped
  almonds
4⅓ tablespoons butter, divided
2 teaspoons poppy seeds

Sprinkle the veal with salt and pepper. Brown it along with the garlic in the salad oil. Add the water. Cover and simmer for 1 hour, or until the meat is tender. Let it cool a few minutes, then remove the garlic and stir in the sour cream and paprika. Reheat gently—don't let it boil—and serve over the noodles.

To make the noodles: Cook the noodles for a little less time than the package says. Drain. Now cook the almonds in 1 teaspoon butter until light brown. Add the remaining butter, then the poppy seeds and the drained noodles. Toss until combined, then reheat carefully, stirring well.
• *SERVES 6.*

All of this, the veal and the noodles, too, can be prepared well in advance and reheated when you're ready to serve. In fact, when I cooked the 360 servings mentioned above, we did it in casserole dishes—60 of them, if you can imagine. Just put the cooked and flavored noodles with their almonds and poppyseeds in the bottom of a baking dish, then cover with the veal mixture. Bake, covered, at 350° F just long enough to heat everything.

Veal Birds with Sage Dressing

Veal birds look like the cute fat quails they are supposed to imitate. I remember thinking it was fun to look at them and imagine they were little birds, and I always thoroughly enjoyed the taste, but they were an everyday dish. With the price of veal these days, this concept may well have changed.

Actually, when I think about it, I can't remember any main courses that were considered fancy. We certainly had our favorite dishes, though, and veal birds ranked right up there with the best of them.

2 tablespoons butter
1 medium onion, finely chopped
¾ cup soft bread crumbs
1 teaspoon sage
Salt and pepper
8 3 x 5-inch slices veal cutlet, pounded until thin
Flour for dredging
3 tablespoons bacon fat (or use half butter, half salad oil)
Water or milk to half cover the birds
1 tablespoon flour for sauce (optional)

Cook the onions in the butter, over medium heat until soft but not browned. Make a stuffing by adding to the onions the bread crumbs, sage and salt and pepper. Divide this among the slices of veal and roll each up, tucking in the ends and tying with string.

Coat the rolls/birds with a little flour and brown them in the bacon fat or butter and oil. Add enough water or milk to come halfway up the sides of the rolls, cover and simmer for about 25 minutes, or until tender.

If you want a sauce, remove the meat rolls and add 1 tablespoon flour to the juices in the pan, cooking and stirring for 3 or 4 minutes. Add a little water or milk and cook down to the desired consistency.
• *SERVES 4 to 8.*

City Chicken

City Chicken isn't chicken at all. It's a very tasty (and quite sophisticated, though probably country-born) veal and pork dish which is supposed to look like chicken drumsticks. The technique used is very French, so this may be derived from settlers from France.

The title is an example of the fun Midwesterners have with their food and with the names given to various dishes. (It sounds like part of some old joke which begins, "Why, those city people are so dumb they think . . .")

1 pound veal steak
1 pound pork
Salt and pepper
Flour for dredging
1 egg, lightly beaten
¾ cup homemade bread crumbs
¼ cup butter or bacon fat
½ cup water

Cut the veal and pork into roughly 1-inch cubes. Impale them alternately on 4 to 6 small skewers. Combine the flour with the salt and pepper. Roll each skewer first in the flour, then the egg, then the bread crumbs. Brown thoroughly over medium heat in the butter or bacon fat in a large frying pan, then add the water, cover the pan and simmer for 30 minutes, or until tender. • *SERVES 4 to 6.*

Bread crumbs are easily made at home by tearing up day-old bread, then running it in a blender or food processor.

Crisp-topped Roast Pork

This is the old-fashioned, Midwestern, absolutely wonderful way of cooking a pork roast. As opposed to the results from the low-temperature-throughout, "modern" way of roasting, you end up with a crackling crisp crust and admirable brown gravy. Pork cooked this way is served just about weekly in many Midwestern households and has been for generations. You'll look a long time before you find a recipe for it, though. I think you're supposed to be born knowing how to cook it, and most Midwesterners probably are.

1 5-pound loin of pork
Salt and pepper

FOR THE GRAVY

2 tablespoons flour
1 cup chicken broth or water

Rub the meat with salt and pepper. Put into a shallow pan, bone side down. (No rack is needed.) Roast, uncovered, at 450° F for 20 minutes, then turn the oven down to 350° F and continue roasting until a meat thermometer registers 180° F—a total of about 30 minutes per pound.
• *SERVES 6 to 8.*

To make the gravy: Remove the meat to a platter. Pour off all but about 3 tablespoons of the fat in the pan. To this, add 2 tablespoons of flour. Cook and stir on top of the stove for a few minutes, letting the flour brown and scraping up all the brown bits in the pan. Now add the chicken broth or water and simmer, stirring or whisking, until thickened. Taste to see if you need additional salt and pepper.

Glazed Roast Loin of Pork with Peaches

This is a fancier way of roasting a loin of pork than the previous recipe, but it's just as Midwestern and just as delicious.

 1 tablespoon flour
 1 teaspoon sage
 ½ teaspoon salt
 1 4-pound loin of boneless pork, rolled and tied
 ¼ teaspoon black pepper
 3 tablespoons honey
 3 tablespoons cider vinegar
 2 tablespoons catsup
 12 peach halves, fresh or canned

Combine the flour, sage, salt and pepper and rub all over the pork. Put on a rack in a shallow pan and bake at 450° F for 15 minutes. Turn the oven down to 350° F and continue roasting, basting often with a combination of the honey, cider vinegar and catsup, until a meat thermometer registers 180° F (about 30 minutes per pound).

About 20 minutes before the roast is done, put the peaches, cut side up, on the rack with the meat. Baste every few minutes with some of the honey–cider vinegar glaze.

To make a sauce, defat the juices in the pan. • *SERVES 6.*

Pork Chops Baked with Cider and Apples

You might think this scrumptious dish of pork chops, apples, cider and cream is French, direct from Normandy. It's not, though. It's a sensible Midwestern combination of ingredients usually available in the fall of the year.

 4 thick pork chops
 ½ teaspoon sage or poultry seasoning
 1 tablespoon butter
 1 cup chopped onion
 4 apples, peeled and sliced
 ¾ cup apple cider (apple juice can be substituted)
 ¼ cup light or heavy cream
 Salt and pepper to taste

Trim off some of the fat from the chops and melt it for 3 to 4 minutes over medium-low heat in a large frying pan. Rub the sage or poultry seasoning into the chops and cook them in the frying pan until browned on both sides. Remove to a baking dish in which they'll fit in one layer.

Melt the butter in the same frying pan. Add the onion and cook gently just until wilted. Now add the apples, cider, cream and salt and pepper and heat slowly to just under the boiling point. Pour over the chops. Cover and bake at 350° F for one hour. • *SERVES 4.*

German Pork Chops Baked in Sour Cream and Lemon Juice

I swoon over these pork chops, and I'm far from alone in this. You've just never tasted a better combination of flavors, or eaten pork that is more tender. I always serve them with baked sweet potatoes, but most people favor rice or mashed potatoes as a side dish.

Be careful when you remove the cover after these chops have cooked. They seem to build up an unusual amount of steam. I once received quite a bad burn because I was so anxious to eat my beloved chops that I yanked the lid off the moment the dish came out of the oven. For this reason, foil makes the best lid for them, since you can poke a hole in it to let the steam escape.

4 medium-thick pork chops
Flour for dredging
1 tablespoon salad oil or lard (or
    melt some of the fat from the
    chops and use that)
¾ cup sour cream
Juice of 1 lemon
Grated rind of ½ lemon
1 teaspoon sugar
¼ teaspoon thyme
2 scallions, minced
Salt and pepper
½ cup water

Lightly coat the chops on both sides with the flour, then brown them slowly in whichever fat you choose to use. Put them in a shallow buttered baking dish. Combine the remaining ingredients and pour over the chops. Bake, covered, at 350° F for 1 hour. • *SERVES 4.*

Stamppot

When I wanted to learn about the descendants of Dutch settlers who live in Holland, Michigan, I wrote to the library there. Back came first a phone call, then a letter with recipes, information and pamphlets, all from a man named Ralph Haan.

Mr. Haan told me that the entire area from Grand Rapids to Lake Michigan is heavily populated with people of Dutch descent. He emphasized the "good work ethic" of these people and told me that while the area is booming, the Dutch heritage is not being forgotten. A recently built shopping center even has orange tile roofs and stepped storefronts reminiscent of those in Holland.

The city of Holland has a six-day Tulip Festival every May, featuring seventy-five to one hundred bands, Dutch costumes and so on. In or near the town are a reconstructed Dutch village, a giant windmill brought over from the Netherlands and even a wooden shoe factory.

Among the recipes Mr. Haan sent me is one from his grandmother for a traditional Dutch stew. He told me that his grandmother called this dish something that sounded like "mouse" and that as a child he was afraid he was about to have to eat mice when it was presented to him. I've learned from other sources that a more usual name for it is stamppot met boeren kool—or just stamppot. Whatever the name, it's a stew made from potatoes, kale and sausage and it's an unexcelled chill chaser for winter evenings. Mr. Haan says to serve it with homemade applesauce. A good idea.

> 6 medium potatoes, peeled and cubed
> 1 pound kale, stripped of its stems, boiled until tender and finely minced (or use canned kale—or turnip greens)
> 1 pound smoked sausage
> 1 medium onion, chopped (optional)
> 2 medium carrots, chopped (optional)
> Salt and pepper to taste

Boil the potatoes in water to half cover until they're falling apart, adding more water if necessary. Now add the kale and sausage and the onion and carrot, if you're using them. Cook gently for about 40 minutes. Season with salt and pepper.

The *stamppot* can be eaten now, but it will be even better if it's kept overnight in the refrigerator and reheated in the oven the next day. • *SERVES 4.*

Spareribs and Sauerkraut

It's hard to think what could be a more basically Midwestern dish than dear old Spareribs and Sauerkraut. And they're so good! The fact that they're also about the easiest thing you could ever cook is simply a nice bonus. Boiled new potatoes, still in their skins, go well with Spareribs and Sauerkraut. You might, in fact, want to bury them in the sauerkraut for at least the last part of their cooking so they'll pick up some extra flavor. Some people get a little carried away and add everything from onions to apples to caraway to juniper berries to their Spareribs and Sauerkraut. Don't. This isn't a fancy choucroute garnie. It's just plain old-fashioned Spareribs and Sauerkraut and it's perfect just the way it is.

2 tablespoons bacon grease or
    other fat
3 pounds spareribs, cut into serving
    pieces
1½ pounds sauerkraut
1 cup water
Salt and pepper

Heat the fat in a large frying pan and brown the spareribs lightly in it. Put the sauerkraut in a baking dish and cover with the spareribs. Pour on the water, sprinkle with salt and pepper and bake, covered, at 350° F for 1½ hours, removing the cover for the last 20 minutes.
• *SERVES 4 to 6.*

Deachie's Barbecued Spareribs

Deachie, my grandmother, loved to experiment in her cooking, but she didn't have much chance to, what with all of us clamoring for such old family favorites as her barbecued spareribs. Some things which make great memories don't hold up well when you reencounter them later in life. Houses you knew in your childhood mysteriously shrink to half their size and so on. These spareribs, though, taste every bit as good now as they did when I was a child.

3 to 4 pounds meaty spareribs
Salt and pepper
2 large onions, halved and thinly
    sliced
2 tablespoons cider vinegar
2 tablespoons Worcestershire sauce
1 cup catsup
¾ teaspoon paprika
¾ teaspoon chili powder
1½ cups water

Sprinkle the ribs with salt and pepper, then put them in a roasting pan. Cover them with the sliced onions, then with all the other ingredients combined. Bake, covered, at 350° F for 1½ hours, basting occasionally. Remove the cover for the last 20 minutes to allow browning. • *SERVES 4 to 6.*

Hickory-flavored Roast Lamb

The hickory flavor in this roast lamb is achieved indoors, not over a wood fire. My mother did this by rubbing a leg of lamb first with lemon juice, then with a commercial "cure" for hams. This gave an enjoyable flavor, but I wouldn't want to use the "cures" these days, even if I had access to them, since they are loaded with chemicals which we've now been told are not exactly conducive to good health.

The sugar in the recipe may be a surprise to the rest of the country, but it's a common touch in the cooking of many Midwestern meats, not just lamb.

1 lemon
1 6- to 7-pound leg of lamb
⅓ cup brown sugar
4 drops Wright's Natural Hickory Seasoning ("liquid smoke"), available in most markets
½ teaspoon salt
¼ teaspoon black pepper

Cut the lemon in half and rub it all over the leg of lamb, squeezing out the juice as you go. Combine all the remaining ingredients and rub well into the lamb.

Put the roast on a rack in a baking pan and cook at 325° F for about 2 hours, or until done to your taste. Don't baste, but do add a little water to the pan from time to time.
• *SERVES 6 to 8.*

I have never seen a meat thermometer in a Midwestern kitchen, though no doubt there are many of them there now. The old ways to tell if a roast was done were by keeping track of how long it had cooked, taking a good look at it to see if it *looked* done and lightly pressing the meat with one's fingers (if it felt firm, it was ready). There were also always those who poked the meat with a long-tined fork to see the color of the juices which ran out, and the heretics who cut off a slice of the meat to look at it, not to mention sneak a taste.

Swedish Roast Lamb with Coffee and Cream

Perhaps you have to be either Swedish or Midwestern to enjoy this roast. The first time I cooked it, I served it to a distant relative of my first husband. This boorish guest's comment was, "It's a shame to ruin a leg of lamb like this." (But since this cousin-in-law had already said that our living room would no doubt be quite attractive if we painted it a different color, I didn't pay too much attention—especially since everyone else enjoyed the lamb and seemed to like our living room just the way it was.)

Salt and pepper to taste
1 6- to 7-pound leg of lamb
2 thickly sliced onions
2 thickly sliced carrots
1 cup strong hot coffee
½ cup light or heavy cream
1 tablespoon sugar
Water (see below)

Rub the salt and pepper into the lamb, then place it on a rack in a baking pan. Strew the onion and carrot slices around the bottom of the pan. Bake at 425° F for 20 minutes, then turn the heat down to 325° F and cook for another 20 minutes. Mix the coffee with the cream and sugar and pour it over the lamb. Bake, basting often with the juices in the pan and adding a little water, if necessary, for half an hour more, or until done as desired.

Remove the lamb to a warm platter. Strain the pan juices and spoon off as much fat as you can, then reheat and use as a gravy.
• *SERVES 6 to 8.*

Irish Stew

Many Irish came to live in the American Midwest in the nineteenth century and later, but their ways of cooking never made a great impact, probably because they were too similar to the simpler dishes already in favor.

This dish is an exception. It's just an honest, basic lamb stew, but it's always called "Irish." Almost everyone makes it.

2 pounds stewing lamb, cut in
    roughly 1½-inch pieces
4 medium potatoes, peeled and
    cut into large cubes
1 large onion, cut into chunks
1 or 2 thickly sliced carrots
1 purple-topped turnip, peeled
    and sliced (optional)
Salt and pepper
Water

Put the lamb and vegetables into a saucepan. Add a little salt and pepper and enough water to cover by about half an inch. Bring to a boil, turn down the heat, cover and simmer for roughly 2 hours, or until the meat is tender.
• *SERVES 4 to 6.*

Savory Lamb Stew with Dill

Irish Stew, the previous recipe, is the basic heartland lamb stew, but the Scandinavians, and any others who prefer food with more piquancy and jazziness, are apt to make this vinegary variation, either on a regular basis or as an occasional surprise for their families. Fortunately, most Midwestern families like surprises of this sort. (In my family, almost anything which contained vinegar was considered mouthwateringly good, to the point where a little cut glass vinegar cruet was usually on the table at meals. As a cousin of my mother's once said, "Vinegar is the curse of this family.")

There are more complicated procedures you can go through when making this stew—but why? The simple way:

Make Irish Stew, the previous recipe, adding toward the end 1½ teaspoons dill weed, 1 tablespoon vinegar and 1 teaspoon sugar. • *SERVES 6 to 8.*

Bacon-Wrapped Lamb Patties

Lamb chops are an expensive cut of meat, and Midwesterners have never been an extravagant bunch. So those who don't raise their own lambs have learned a fine way to simulate chops at a fraction of the cost.

Old-time cooks always served lamb well-done, but the Eastern heresy of rare or at least "pink" lamb has spread to the younger cooks in the heartland, who enjoy the added juiciness.

Since I prefer "pink" lamb myself, that's what this recipe tells you to make. For well-done, simply cook the patties over lower heat from the beginning.

1⅓ pounds lean ground lamb
4 slices bacon

Form the ground lamb into 4 fat patties. Wrap a strip of bacon around each of these and secure it with a toothpick. (Don't wrap the bacon too tightly; you want a little slack, since it will shrink as it cooks.)

Heat a large frying pan over fairly high heat, then brown the patties on both sides. At this point you have very rare lamb and downright raw bacon. So turn the heat down and place each patty up on edge, propped up against the edge of the pan so it won't fall over. Cook for a little bit, then roll the patties along, still on edge, so another part of the bacon can cook. Keep this up until the whole strip of bacon on each patty is cooked. (Believe it or not, this is fun. It also doesn't take long.)

Drain for a moment on paper towels before serving. • *SERVES 4.*

Baked "Country" Ham

It's very hard to find a real country ham these days (but see page 209 for a few sources), and when you do find one, it's even harder to pay for it. Too bad, too, because, although they're great, they cost several times the going price of supermarket hams. But there's a happy ending to this sad story: You can make a supermarket ham have almost the taste and texture of country ham, and very easily, too. The trick is to cook out all the excess water the manufacturers seem to feel it necessary to add to ham while it's being processed. All slipperiness disappears, and the ham becomes tender but firm.

Buy a half or whole regular, bone-in, ready-to-eat ham. Put in a shallow baking pan, fat side up, and bake it, undisturbed, at 300° F for at least 4 to 5 hours for a half a ham or up to 8 hours for a whole ham.

Now pour off the accumulated water in the pan—there'll be a lot of it—and remove the skin. Score the fat into diamonds, stud each with a clove and pat brown sugar all over the top of the ham. Turn the oven up to 375° F and put the ham back in for about 20 minutes, or until the brown sugar has glazed.

Let the ham sit at room temperature for at least an hour before slicing thin and serving. • *SERVES 6 to 8 with leftovers.*

Ham with Potatoes and Green Beans

Unless your ham has been served for an immense gathering, there's going to be quite a bit left. That's one of the points of having it in the first place, to have the wherewithal to make some well-loved dishes. Of course, the ham can (and does) reappear just plain sliced or in sandwiches, or slivers of it can be added to soups and potatoes, but it's at its finest in such simple dishes as this and the ones that follow.

2 cups diced ham
2 cups potatoes, peeled and
   cubed
2 cups green beans, topped and
   tailed and cut into 1-inch pieces
Water
Mustard

Put the ham, potatoes and green beans in a fairly large saucepan. Cover amply with water and simmer until the vegetables are done. Now boil the water down until it has almost disappeared and stir in some of your best mustard. Not something fancy like a Dijon, but a hot and sweet mustard such as the one on page 203. Since it's rather hot, use only about a teaspoon. If you use a milder, store-bought mustard, use more, up to about a tablespoon. • *SERVES 4.*

Amana German-style Pickled Ham

I was thrilled to learn that the magnificent hams and bacon that my grandfather used to take me to Amana, Iowa, to buy are still available (see page 209).

"In the 1850s, a group of German immigrants settled in a lush river valley in east central Iowa. They were members of a small but dedicated religious following. . . . They called their new home Amana from a passage in the Song of Solomon that means 'to remain faithful.'

They have remained faithful to this day; faithful in their commitment to the quality of life, and to the pure and simple pleasures that make the good life worth living. Pride in workmanship. A home in the heartland. And sharing good food with good friends."

Those glowing words, which actually express everything I've been saying in this book, are from the brochure of the Amana Meat Shop and Smokehouse. This is their recipe for a very nice cold dish, salad, snack or appetizer. As you see, it's for using up the last bits of ham, but it's worth doing with, say, diced ham steak.

Remove bits of ham from the bone and dice in small pieces. Marinate in the refrigerator overnight in a combination of half vinegar and half water, along with some slices of onion. The Amana people also suggest adding some pimiento "for color."

Honeyed Ham with Parsnips

If you've never tried parsnips, traditionally one of the standbys of winter Midwestern cooking, you're in for a surprise. Most people expect them to have a turnip flavor, but this is not true. Especially fixed this way, they're sweet and very, very pleasant. Be sure to use young, fairly small parsnips; they do not improve with age.

1½ pounds ham, cut into 1-inch cubes
⅛ teaspoon ground cloves
⅛ teaspoon nutmeg
2 tablespoons water
2 tablespoons cider vinegar
½ cup honey
2½ cups peeled parsnips, cut into ½-inch slices
Salt

Place the cubes of ham in a covered baking dish or Dutch oven. Combine the ground cloves, nutmeg, water, cider vinegar and honey and pour over the ham. Bake at 325° F, covered, for 45 minutes. Place the parsnips in a saucepan with water to cover and a bit of salt. Bring to a boil, turn down the heat and cook until just tender, partially covered, about 5 minutes. Drain. Remove the baking dish from the oven, top with the parsnips and return to the oven, uncovered, until the top is brown and the liquid has mostly disappeared. • *SERVES 4 to 6.*

Honey-fried Ham Slices

My mother invented this way of cooking ham slices quite accidentally, but the effect it gives is reminiscent of Midwestern ways.

We were in the middle of moving, a dreadful exercise which has punctuated my life too frequently in my childhood and ever since. Our first night in the new place, with the boxes of kitchen things mostly unpacked, Mother bravely set out to cook dinner. She had some sliced ham, so she decided to fry it in a little bacon fat. Too late to change things, she discovered that what she thought was the usual can of bacon fat near the stove was, instead, a can of honey. The result was so delicious that she often cooked slices of ham this way ever after. Me, too.

Do you need a recipe? Just put some honey in a frying pan, add thin-sliced ham and cook, turning the slices often, until glazed.

Ham Steak Baked in Milk and Mustard

This is one of the few ham dishes which doesn't start off as a way to use leftover baked ham. You actually go out and buy a ham steak for it.

The milk tenderizes the meat as it cooks and forms a delectable, slightly browned topping.

1 ham steak, about 1½ inches thick
Water (optional—see below)
¼ cup brown sugar
2 teaspoons dry mustard
1 cup milk
1 pinch baking soda

If you want to get rid of some of the salt in the ham, blanch it by covering it with cold water and bringing the water to a boil. Drain.

Put the ham, blanched or not, in a baking pan just a little bigger than it is. Spread with a mixture of the brown sugar and mustard. Combine the milk and baking soda and carefully add to the pan. There should be just enough liquid to barely cover the ham; if there's not enough, add a little more milk.

Bake at 375° F for 1 hour. • *SERVES 4.*

Glazed Individual Ham Loaves

Ham loaves have always been popular in the heartland. One fairly small cookbook from a church group in Iowa contains nineteen recipes for them! It isn't just that this is a helpful way to use up leftover ham. The main things are that ham loaves make fine eating and lend themselves to a cook's ingenuity. (Practically anything can be and is added to them. Some of the ingredients in those nineteen recipes: Tapioca; tomato juice or purée or soup; green pepper; raisins; cracker crumbs; ground pork, veal or sausage; cloves; peas; pineapple; mustard; cornflakes; celery; Worcestershire sauce; maraschino cherries; grated cheese; cooked rice.)

Here's my personal favorite of the Midwestern ham loaves:

1 pound ground ham
1 pound sausage meat
1/4 cup minced onion
1 egg, lightly beaten
1/3 cup cracker crumbs
3/4 cup cider or apple juice
Salt and pepper to taste
2 tablespoons flour
3/4 cup brown sugar
2 tablespoons vinegar (especially tarragon vinegar)
1/2 teaspoon prepared mustard

Combine the ham, sausage meat, onion, egg, cracker crumbs, cider or apple juice and salt and pepper. Shape into 6 oval loaves, sprinkle each with a teaspoon of flour and place them on a baking sheet. Bake at 375° F for 25 minutes.

Meanwhile, mix the brown sugar, vinegar and mustard in a small pan and bring to a boil. Cook for about 30 seconds, then remove from the heat.

When the loaves have baked for 25 minutes, sprinkle each of them with half of the brown sugar glaze. Put back in the oven for 5 minutes, then sprinkle on the rest of the glaze. Bake for 3 to 4 minutes more.
• *SERVES 6.*

The tarragon vinegar often used in the glaze for these ham loaves is not some fancy French variety. Mr. Heinz makes a malt vinegar flavored with tarragon that's been used for many years in dishes such as this.

Sweet-and-Sour Meat Loaf

Meat loaf started out as something dear to the hearts of Midwesterners, a "meat stretcher." The rise in price of ground meat has tarnished that image a bit, but it's still a beloved dish.

Many of the meat loaves made in the heartland contain not only beef but also veal and pork. This is impractical if you're making a smallish loaf, though. (Try asking a modern supermarket butcher for a third of a pound of this and a half a pound of that and three-quarters of a pound of the other thing.) Nowadays, almost everyone uses just beef.

For a remarkable sandwich, try using sliced cold meat loaf with chili sauce (page 204) or Red Pepper Relish (page 198) on homemade white bread. It's enough to make you take up brown bagging.

1½ pounds ground beef
½ cup soft bread crumbs
1 egg, lightly beaten
¼ cup milk
1 medium-size onion, finely
   chopped
2 carrots, grated or minced
1 clove garlic, pressed or very
   finely minced
1 teaspoon Worcestershire sauce
Salt and pepper to taste

Combine all the ingredients and put into a loaf pan. Bake at 350° F for 1½ hours. Allow to sit for about 10 minutes before slicing. • *SERVES 4 with some left over for sandwiches.*

Crisp Brown Hash

Browned hash is a fitting farewell appearance not only for corned beef but also for any cooked meat or poultry. This is the sort of dish for which you're not supposed to need a recipe, so I'll just sketch in the outlines for you. There's nothing to it.

The three main ingredients are already cooked meat or poultry of any sort, potatoes and onions. The potatoes can be raw or cooked, peeled or not. The onions are raw. The proportions are up to you, but it's usual to have more meat than anything else and more potato than onion. Chop these ingredients quite small or put them through a meat grinder. (Or if you have a food processor, your hash is half made.)

Melt 2 or 3 tablespoons of butter or other fat in a frying pan. Add the ground or chopped mixture. Sprinkle with salt and pepper. Cook over fairly low heat, letting the hash brown a bit, but stirring often. When the hash is cooked, in about 25 minutes, press it down firmly and cook a bit more until a brown bottom crust has formed. A little light or heavy cream added toward the end of the cooking process helps the browning and eliminates any possible dryness.

Serve with catsup or the chili sauce on page 204 or the Red Pepper Relish on page 198.

Poultry

and

Game

Midwestern chicken, ducks and turkeys must be fed with the region's famous field corn, because they're not only plump and delicious but also yellow-skinned. And oh, the wonderful ways they're cooked!

Midwestern game is legendary. Today, as in the past, it's mainly the men who shoot it and, in most cases, clean it. Then, usually by women but nowadays sometimes by an occasional clever man, it's cooked in the simple ways of long ago. It's a treasure, and is treated as such.

Country-fried Chicken with Cream Gravy

Proud though they are of their home cooking, Midwesterners are fond of going to restaurants from time to time. Most towns had their small Chinese restaurants offering chop suey and chow mein, and Greek immigrants started restaurants all over the place. (Not, of course, that they served Greek food in them.)

My own favorite Iowa restaurant in the 1940s had no name and no sign and was only open for one meal a week—Sunday midday dinner. It only served one thing, too—an unbelievably good fried chicken dinner. You had to know about this restaurant by word of mouth, obviously. It was located just over the railroad tracks in the so-small-it-was-almost-invisible town of Middletown, on the highway to Burlington, and it looked just like any other white frame Iowa farmhouse, the sort you'd almost expect to see Grant Wood characters standing in front of.

We'd go there straight from church at about noon. Inside the house, the double front parlor furniture had been replaced with tables and chairs, at least for this one day a week. There were starched white tablecloths and friendly women to serve you. There were bowls of corn relish and such on the tables, and in would come heaping platters of country-fried chicken, mashed potatoes, biscuits, cream gravy, corn fritters—and I forget what else. (What else could truly matter?) There was no doubt at least coleslaw for a side dish and apple pie for dessert.

This is how to make a comparable country-fried chicken and its cream gravy. It's a worthy foundation for a restaurant, though in this day of boards of health keeping an eye on everything, it might be hard to operate it in a farmhouse.

¾ cup flour
Salt, pepper and paprika
2 frying chickens, cut-up
½ cup fat for frying—bacon fat,
    lard, butter, oil or a combination
1 cup (or a bit more) milk

Mix the ½ cup flour in a bag (a brown grocery bag is traditional and very effective) with some salt, pepper and paprika. Shake the chicken in this, a few pieces at a time, until well coated. (Save the flour for later.)

Heat whatever fat you choose (the more flavorful the fat, the better the taste of the chicken) in a large frying pan or iron skillet. When the fat is almost smoking, start adding the floured pieces of chicken. When one side is brown, turn the pieces over and turn the heat down a little. As the pieces become brown on that side, too, remove them to an open pan in a 350° F oven. (This not only keeps the chicken hot until you want to serve it but also helps make it crisp.)

Pour off all but about 2 tablespoons of the fat. Add 2 tablespoons of the seasoned flour from the bag and stir until lightly brown, scraping up all the little morsels on the bottom of the pan. Add the milk and continue stirring until the gravy thickens. If it becomes too thick, add a bit more milk. Taste to see if it needs any salt and pepper.

Serve with the chicken—and with biscuits and mashed potatoes. • *SERVES 6 to 8.*

Chicken Smothered with Onions

Here is one of the most mouthwatering of all Midwestern recipes. The secret ingredient is lard. You can use other fats, but the result won't be quite the same.

4 chicken quarters
Salt, pepper and paprika
2 tablespoons lard
⅓ cup water
2 cups thin-sliced onions

Sprinkle the chicken quarters with a little salt, pepper and paprika. Melt the lard over medium-high heat in a large frying pan with a lid (a large electric frying pan, for instance). Add the chicken and cook, turning occasionally, until brown.

Turn down the heat, add the water and cover the pan. Simmer for about half an hour, or until tender.

Now remove the lid, turn the heat up a bit and cook off most of the liquid in the pan. At this point, add the onions and cook, stirring frequently, for 10 to 15 minutes, or until light brown. • *SERVES 4.*

Indiana Chicken Paprikash

The Midwesterners of Hungarian origin, especially those in Indiana, call this dish "Chicken Paprikash." Elsewhere, in other groups, it's known as Chicken Paprika or even just Chicken in Sour Cream. By any name, it's terrific.

½ cup chopped onions
3 tablespoons butter or other fat
1 3-pound chicken, cut into serving
    pieces
2 teaspoons paprika (Hungarian, if
    possible)
2 cups chicken broth (see page 51)
1 cup sour cream
Salt and pepper

Using a large frying pan with a lid, cook the chopped onions in the fat over medium-low heat for 3 to 4 minutes. Stir in the paprika and cook for 2 to 3 minutes more, then add the broth and stir until smooth and hot. Now put the chicken pieces in the pan, cover and cook over low heat for about 1½ hours, or until tender. Allow to cool a bit, then stir in the sour cream and season with the salt and pepper. Reheat gently, Serve on noodles. • *SERVES 4.*

Deviled Chicken

Most Midwestern households have a recipe of this sort in the cook's file or notebook, and the dish is much appreciated not only for itself but also for the ease with which it is made. This particular Deviled Chicken is based on one in Bach for More, *one of the cookbooks put out by the Junior Committee of the Cleveland (Ohio) Orchestra. Theirs uses Dijon mustard and adds ½ teaspoon tarragon to the butter mixture. While that's the way I usually make it myself, it's much more typically Midwestern to use American-style mustard and omit the pleasantly pungent herb.*

¼ cup prepared mustard (Dijon or
    other)
2 tablespoons minced onion
A dash of Tabasco sauce or
    cayenne
5 tablespoons butter, melted,
    divided
1 3-pound chicken, quartered
¾ cup soft, homemade bread
    crumbs

Combine the mustard, onion and Tabasco or cayenne with 1 tablespoon of the melted butter and use this to coat the chicken pieces. Roll each piece in the bread crumbs, patting in well, then put in a baking pan. Pour the rest of the melted butter on top of each piece.

Bake at 375° F for 1 hour or a little more, until the crumbs are brown and the chicken done. • *SERVES 4.*

Boiled Chicken

A high percentage of Midwestern chicken recipes call for already cooked chicken, and this is the best way to get it. The meat will be tender and full of flavor. One sound idea, if you're cooking for just, say, four to six people, is to serve half the chicken the day you cook it, accompanied by gravy, then refrigerate or freeze the other cooked half until you want it for some such dish as chicken salad. This is also the recipe to use to obtain fine chicken broth; it will keep, frozen, for a long time.

　1 5-pound stewing chicken or fowl, cut up
　1 stalk celery, cut in 3-inch pieces
　1 carrot, cut in 2-inch pieces
　1 onion, stuck with 2 cloves
　4 whole peppercorns
　Salt to taste

FOR THE CHICKEN GRAVY

　3 tablespoons chicken fat or butter
　2 tablespoons flour
　1½ cups strained chicken broth
　Salt and pepper to taste

Put the chicken, vegetables and peppercorns in a large pot (or use a Crockpot). Add enough water to cover. Simmer, covered, (don't boil) until the chicken is tender. This will probably take 2½ to 3 hours. Add salt only after the first hour of cooking.

To make the chicken gravy:　Melt the chicken fat or butter in a saucepan. Add the flour and cook, stirring, until the flour just begins to brown. Now add the strained broth from the chicken and cook, still stirring, until thickened. Taste to see if it needs salt and pepper.

Chicken and Noodles

This dish is probably the Midwestern grandmother of Chicken alla Tetrazzini, a sophisticated Eastern creation named in honor of a famous opera singer. You'll find Tetrazzini, with its sherry and egg yolks and mushrooms and such, in many cookbooks, but you won't often find Chicken and Noodles. It's too simple, no doubt—but, confidentially, this is the better dish.

　8 ounces medium-thin noodles
　4 cups chicken broth
　2 to 3 cups diced cooked chicken
　½ cup light or heavy cream, sweet or sour
　Salt and pepper to taste

Boil the noodles gently in the chicken broth for about 6 minutes, stirring often. Let sit for 10 minutes—all or almost all the broth should be absorbed by the noodles. Add the chicken and cream and reheat slowly, stirring. Season with salt and pepper.
• *SERVES 4 to 6.*

Chicken Fricassee with Drop Dumplings

This is from a recipe handwritten about sixty-five years ago in Illinois, but it's the sort of well-loved thing still done for, say, a Sunday dinner in the Midwest. (The origin of the name and the general concept of the dish are French, but the result is pure heartland.)

4 pounds chicken, cut up
Salt and pepper
Flour for dredging
3 tablespoons bacon fat or other
    shortening
Boiling water (see below)

FOR THE DUMPLINGS

2 cups flour
4 teaspoons baking powder
½ teaspoon salt
2 teaspoons lard or other
    shortening
About ¾ cup milk

TO FINISH

1 tablespoon butter
1 tablespoon flour

Sprinkle the pieces of chicken with salt and pepper, then dredge them with flour. Cook them in a large frying pan in the bacon fat or other shortening until brown, then put them in a fairly deep covered saucepan. (A Dutch oven would work well—the original recipe called for a kettle—or you could use a Crockpot.)

Add enough boiling water to cover, then put the lid on tightly and simmer for about 2 hours, or until the chicken is tender.

To make the dumplings: Combine the flour, baking powder and salt. Rub the shortening in with your fingers (or be modern and use a food processor). Add just enough milk to make the mixture hold together. Drop by tablespoons on top of the chicken, not into the gravy (this is important). Cover tightly and steam for 12 minutes without peeking.

Remove the chicken and dumplings, then thicken the gravy with a mixture of the butter and flour and cook and stir for 4 to 5 minutes. • *SERVES 6 to 8.*

Chicken with Rolled Dumplings

When I crave chicken with dumplings, it's rolled dumplings I have in mind. Rolled dumplings are not at all like steamed dumplings. They have more the texture of pasta, and they're imbued through and through with the taste of chicken.

1 4- to 5-pound stewing chicken or fowl, cooked by the recipe on page 51
Chicken gravy from the same recipe

FOR THE DUMPLINGS

1 cup flour
1½ teaspoons baking powder
½ teaspoon salt
2 tablespoons butter or lard
About ½ cup milk

When the chicken is cooked, remove 1½ cups of its broth to make the gravy (see page 51). Make sure there's at least a cup of broth remaining in the pot with the chicken. If not, add some water.

To make the dumplings: Combine the flour, baking powder and salt and cut in the butter or lard. Add just enough milk to make a rollable mixture. Roll out on a floured surface until quite thin—between ⅛ and ¼ inch. Cut into strips or elongated diamond shapes, roughly 1 × 2 or 3 inches. Put these on top of the chicken, not in the broth. Cover the pot tightly. Bring to a boil,

turn down the heat and simmer for 15 minutes. Serve the chicken and dumplings topped with the gravy. • *SERVES 6 to 8.*

Chicken Hash with Cream

Although I've given a recipe elsewhere (on page 45) for a hash which I said, quite rightly, could be made with "already cooked meat or poultry of any sort," there's a special, much appreciated delicacy to this Chicken Hash with Cream.

¼ cup minced onion
2 tablespoons butter
2 cups cut-up (but not finely) boiled chicken
1 tablespoon flour
1 cup light cream
Salt and pepper to taste
½ cup Parmesan cheese (optional)

Cook the onion in the butter for a few minutes, until limp, then stir in the flour. Cook for 3 or 4 minutes, then add the cream and the cup-up chicken. Cook, stirring, for a few more minutes, or until thickened. Season with salt and pepper.

The hash is excellent right now, but some people put it in a small, buttered baking dish, sprinkle on the grated cheese and put it under a broiler until brown.
• *SERVES 4 to 6.*

Midwestern Chicken Pot Pie

Midwestern Chicken Pot Pie bears very little resemblance to the frozen pies you can find in any supermarket. It usually has a biscuit topping rather than one of piecrust. It has absolutely no artificial ingredients. The chicken meat in it is juicy, and there's a lot of it. Best of all, the taste of the pie is rich and lovely.

Sometimes the pies are made from already boiled chicken and broth, but for a true Midwestern pot pie, start with a fresh fowl.

1 4- to 5-pound stewing chicken, cut up, freshly cooked as in Boiled Chicken (page 51)
1 large potato, peeled, diced and boiled
4 medium carrots, peeled, diced and boiled
½ cup peas, cooked (optional)
6 tablespoons butter or rendered chicken fat
6 tablespoons flour
3 cups chicken broth, produced by boiling the chicken
Salt and pepper to taste

FOR THE TOPPING

2 cups flour
2 teaspoons baking powder
1½ teaspoons salt
1 cup light cream
2 eggs, lightly beaten

Remove the skin and bones from the chicken and cut the meat into large bite-size pieces. Put into a large, well-buttered casserole along with the cooked potatoes, carrots and, if you're using them, the peas. Now make a sauce by melting the butter or chicken fat, adding the flour and stirring for several minutes until it just begins to brown. Add the broth, then cook and stir until it thickens and comes to a boil. Add to the chicken meat and vegetables in the casserole. Season with salt and pepper.

To make the topping: Combine the flour, baking powder and salt. Now quickly and deftly, using as few strokes as possible, stir in the cream and eggs. Spoon this mixture over the combination in the casserole.

Bake at 375° F for 45 minutes, or until golden brown. (For a smaller pie, cut all the ingredients in half.) • *SERVES 8 to 10.*

Lill's Curried Hawaiian Chicken

I've been to a luncheon at the Harlan House Hotel in Mount Pleasant, Iowa, where my Aunt Lill served her Curried Hawaiian Chicken. (A friend of ours owned the hotel, so we were allowed to bring in our own food for parties.) Such oo-ing and ah-ing from happy eaters you've never heard. Midwesterners have never been among the first to try such outlandish combinations as curry powder and fresh pineapple, but once they're introduced to them, watch out! This became a famous and much imitated dish, and for good reason. Many people substitute canned pineapple for fresh, but that's the way life goes.

4 onions, chopped
3 tablespoons salad oil
5 tablespoons flour
1 quart of the chicken broth
    created while boiling the chicken
1 5-pound chicken, cooked as in
    Boiled Chicken (page 51),
    skinned, deboned and cut into
    small pieces
½ teaspoon lemon juice
1 cup diced fresh pineapple
½ cup raisins
2 to 4 teaspoons curry powder
    (I think Lill used 4 teaspoons when
    cooking for the family—we were
    a bold bunch—and 2 teaspoons
    when it was for outside
    consumption)
1½ cups light cream
Fried noodles (the Chinese sort,
    available in supermarkets)

Cook the onions in the oil until well wilted, then add the flour and stir until lightly browned. Add the chicken broth and simmer for 5 minutes. Now add the chicken pieces, lemon juice, pineapple, raisins, curry powder and cream. Simmer for just 3 to 4 minutes.

Serve hot, with the fried noodles as an accompaniment. (Lill's recipe says to serve in covered ramekins, but any serving dish will do just as well.) • *SERVES 12.*

Pressed Chicken

This excellent cold dish of chicken in a sort of self-made aspic has been a standby in the heartland for many years, but it could easily pass for an elegant French-inspired aspic. In fact, it may indeed have originated with some of the French who settled in the area. This particular recipe, though, is adapted from one from Kansas. It's an ideal main dish for any hot summer's day.

Boil a 5-pound chicken by the recipe on page 51, but continue cooking until the meat falls off the bone. Remove the chicken from the broth and allow it to cool, then dice the meat. Skim off any excess fat from the top of the broth, then boil the broth down until it's reduced by about half. Combine the broth with the pieces of chicken, then season to taste.

Pack this mixture into one or more (depending on size) loaf pans. Now to "press" it: Put another loaf pan of the same size on top of each filled pan. Weight it down either with heavy cans or by filling it with water. Refrigerate for at least 8 hours.
• *SERVE, sliced, to 6 or 8.*

Roast Turkey with Corn Bread Stuffing

Probably because of my mother's, my grandmother's, and my own love of experimenting, or at least being adventurous while cooking, I've developed a small mental block about cooking turkey. Every year, especially when cooking for Thanksgiving and/or Christmas with Katie, my older daughter (who shares this family blight), I do the turkey differently. One year, it's doused with wine and securely encased in foil. Another year, it's topped with a large, thin slice of salt pork, and so on. You wouldn't believe some of the ingredients we have put in our stuffings. They range from water chestnuts to pineapple, and from poppy seeds to ginger marmalade. They were all not bad at all, too!

But now I've finally had the sense to turn back to the basic, good old Midwestern way, which turns out a perfect bird.

1 12- to 16-pound turkey, never frozen
Salt and pepper
1 cup butter (more or less), divided
1 cup chopped onion
1 cup chopped celery
1 teaspoon poultry seasoning
1 batch corn bread (see page 145), cooled and crumbled
4 cups homemade white bread crumbs
½ cup (or more) chicken or turkey broth

Rub the turkey, inside and out, with salt and pepper. Melt ½ cup of the butter and cook the onion and celery gently until limp. Add the poultry seasoning, then combine with the crumbled corn bread and white bread crumbs. Moisten with broth and perhaps a little more melted butter if the stuffing seems too dry.

Stuff the turkey lightly in both cavities. (If there's too much stuffing, put some in a small dish to be baked separately.) Truss the bird and secure the openings to keep the stuffing in, then rub all over the outside with soft butter.

Put the bird on a rack in a roasting pan and cover the top loosely with a sheet of foil. (Or do as they used to in the heartland before the advent of foil and cover the top of the turkey with a piece of cloth or several layers of cheesecloth, soaked in butter.)

Roast at 325° F for 4½ to 5½ hours (depending on the bird's size), or until it reaches an internal temperature of 185° F. Baste about every half hour, and remove the foil or cloth for the last half hour so the skin can brown.

For the gravy: As the turkey roasts, cook the giblets and the neck in about 1 quart of water along with 1 cut-up onion, a stalk of celery and a little salt and pepper. If you want a giblet gravy (which I don't), strain off the broth and chop the gizzards. When the bird is done, remove it to a platter and pour off all but approximately 4 tablespoons of the fat in the pan. Stir in 4 tablespoons of flour and cook, stirring, for 3 to 4 minutes, or until light brown. Now add 2 cups of the broth—and the chopped giblets, if you're using them—and cook and stir for another few minutes.

Roast Duckling with Currant Sauce

I'm occasionally asked, "What is your favorite food?" My answer is always that it changes from time to time, even from day to day, depending on what I've been eating. Roast duck is always in my top ten, though, particularly if it's cooked in this simple Midwestern way and served with this marvelous sauce.

Some—but not I—prefer their duck stuffed. If you do, use the turkey stuffing recipe on page 56, omitting the corn bread and using orange juice instead of broth to moisten. You can also add sections of 1 orange, chopped.

The duck does not need to be turned while cooking or pricked with a fork—the fat will run out all by itself, and should, of course, be saved for other cooking.

1 5-pound domestic duck
1 lemon, cut in half
Salt and pepper
1 orange

FOR THE SAUCE

4 tablespoons butter
1½ tablespoons cider vinegar
1 cup currant jelly
½ teaspoon prepared mustard
Salt and cayenne pepper to taste
   (just a bit of the latter)

Remove any visible fat from the vent and the inside of the duck. Rub the lemon halves over the inside and outside of the bird, squeezing out juice as you go, then rub everything with salt and pepper. Slice the orange and stuff it inside the duck. Put the bird on a rack in a baking pan and cook at 350° F for 2 hours, undisturbed. Remove from the oven and let the bird sit for 20 minutes before carving.

To make the sauce: Melt the butter in a small saucepan, then add the cider vinegar, jelly and mustard. Heat gently, stirring, to just below the boiling point, then season to taste with salt and cayenne.

• *SERVES 2 to 4.*

Minnesota Roast Goose with Fruit Stuffing

This recipe is only for a domestic goose, the sort you buy, not one shot by a friend. (Wild goose can take close to forever to become tender. One year my mother and I attempted to cook a Canada goose for Christmas. Dinner ended up being at 10:30 that night, and even then it was a tough old bird we served.)

The Swedes and the Germans probably brought with them the old-world idea that prunes and other fruits cut the fattiness of goose and add a lot of flavor.

This is not an old method of cooking goose (the old ones call for much pricking of the goose and the like), but it defats the bird, gives a crisp skin and is generally superb.

1 10-pound domestic goose

FOR THE STUFFING

1 large onion, chopped,
2 large apples, peeled and chopped
3 stalks celery, finely chopped
4 tablespoons butter
½ cup raisins
1½ cups minced dried prunes or apricots (or a combination)
8 cups dry, homemade bread crumbs or bread cubes
1 teaspoon dried tarragon
½ teaspoon dried thyme
Salt and pepper to taste

Rub only the inside of the goose with salt. Remove any extraneous bits and pieces (lungs, for instance) that shouldn't be there and also any loose pieces of fat.

To make the stuffing: Cook the onion, apples and celery gently in the butter until soft. Add all the other ingredients. Stuff the goose with this and truss it. Put in a baking pan on a rack and cook for 1 hour at 400° F, frequently getting rid of the fat that accumulates in the pan. (Save it for other uses, though.) Don't baste.

Turn the oven down to 350° F and cook for another hour, still removing fat from the pan. Next, turn the heat down to 325° F and cook for from 45 minutes to 1 hour more. The goose will be done when it's a radiant brown and when you poke a fork into a thigh, the juices run clear.

• *SERVES 6 to 8.*

Hasenpfeffer

The rabbits cooked these days in the heartland and elsewhere are mainly farm raised, thus tender and easy to cook. In the old days, though, wild rabbits were shot or trapped for the table and were extremely tough. German immigrants taught their neighbors how to tenderize them and create at the same time a terrific dish. It's now used with store-bought rabbits as well as wild.

1 cup vinegar
1 cup water
1 large onion, sliced
½ teaspoon salt
1 bay leaf
6 black peppercorns
3 whole cloves
1 rabbit, cleaned and cut into serving pieces
3 tablespoons butter, salad oil or other fat
1 cup sour cream

Combine the vinegar, water, onion, salt, bay leaf, peppercorns and cloves and marinate the cut-up rabbit in the mixture for 2 days. Now remove the rabbit pieces from the marinade and brown in the fat in a large frying pan with a lid. Add enough of the marinade to cover and simmer, covered, for 30 minutes. Stir in the sour cream just before serving and taste to see if you need to add more salt. • *SERVES 4.*

Craig's Venison Pie

Most cookbooks tell you that venison must be served rare. This is all very well and good when it's farm-raised venison, but in the heartland, most of the venison cooked is from deer shot by local hunters. The cooks usually don't know the age of the deer and therefore the degree of tenderness. And, believe me, nothing is worse than over-age venison steaks served rare. I've been served venison that was totally unchewable. (Not in the Midwest, but in one of New York's fanciest restaurants.) Terrible!

So the best solution is a stew or, better yet, a pie. Not one that could possibly be confused with an ordinary beef stew or pie, but a very special one such as this. (For a venison stew, just omit the crust.)

1 pound venison, cut into small cubes
2 cloves garlic, whole
1 tablespoon salad oil or olive oil
2 medium onions, sliced
8 ounces mushrooms (whole if very small, sliced if larger)
1 cup red wine (or the juice of 1 lemon plus ¾ cup water)
Salt and pepper to taste
Pie pastry for a 1-crust pie (see page 162)
Currant jelly for serving (optional)

Brown the venison and garlic in the oil, then add the onions and mushrooms. Continue cooking until the onions are soft. Now add the wine or lemon juice and water and the salt and pepper and simmer over low heat for about 30 minutes, or until the meat is tender and the liquid has almost disappeared. (If the meat is still tough at this stage, add a little more water and continue cooking, checking frequently.)

Put into a 1- or 1½-quart buttered baking dish, leaving at least ½ inch of headroom at the top. Top with the crust. Crimp it, then poke it several times with a fork to create steam vents. Put on a baking sheet and bake at 450° F for 10 minutes, then turn the heat down to 350° F and cook for 25 minutes more, or until the crust is golden brown. Serve with currant jelly on the side. (This is optional, but there are many people who feel currant jelly is obligatory with venison.) • *SERVES 4 to 6.*

Wild Duck "Done to a Turn"

When we visited our friends Carlynn and George Brook, who lived near Lake Erie, Carlynn told me a secret. We were about to go out on their boat for the afternoon, and she had planned to have wild ducks, shot previously by George, for dinner.

"I just put a little apple and onion in the ducks and put them in the oven," she said. "Then, no matter how long we're away and the ducks cook—two hours, four hours, it doesn't matter—when I serve them, George always says, 'Done to a turn, Carlynn.'"

And she was right. George did indeed say, "Done to a turn, Carlynn." He was right, too. They couldn't have been better.

If you want to get rid of any fishy flavor or "gaminess" of the ducks—and this is not a bad idea—clean the ducks, then soak them for most of a day in cold, salted water, changing the water a time or two.

Dry the ducks, then stuff each with a small apple and an onion, each cut in half. Cover the breasts with slices of bacon (this is optional—Carlynn didn't do it—but it helps the ducks to self-baste.)

Put into an open roasting pan and bake at 300° F for at least 2 hours, or until you return from whatever adventures you have in mind. • *SERVES 2.*

Old Hunters' Roast Pheasant

Pheasant became so common in the heartland that great (to my way of thinking, anyway) liberties were sometimes taken with it. It was fricasseed, made into stews and even braised with sauerkraut. Unfortunately, in these methods, the pheasant's own lovely and delicate flavor becomes lost (although for a very old pheasant, fricasseeing may be the only possible choice).

If you have very young pheasants, you can broil them as you would chicken. For a somewhat more mature bird, roasting's best. Because it's dry, though, you have to add some fat. (If you have no idea of the age of your pheasants, look for these clues: Younger birds will have white fat and soft breastbones; in older ones, the fat will be yellow and the breastbone stiff.)

Here's how the old hunters would tell you to proceed: Rub the inside of the pheasant well with butter. Truss the legs together as you would a chicken or turkey, then cover the breasts with a thin layer of salt pork or fatty bacon. Roast at 375° F for 40 minutes, basting often with the fat in the pan, then remove the salt pork or bacon and roast for 10 minutes, basting even more vigorously.
• *SERVES 2.*

Roasted Quail

When my grandfather once sent me a boxful of tiny quail, packed in dry ice, I had to make a phone call to the Midwest to find out how to cook them. My friends raved about them and envied me my heartland connections. Here's the system:

Put a little salt and pepper and a tablespoon of butter in the cavity of each bird, then rub the outside of the birds well with more softened butter and sprinkle with more salt and pepper. Put the birds on a rack in a baking pan and roast at 450° F for 20 to 25 minutes, or until brown, basting once. • *SERVE 1 or 2 quails per person.*

Donna's Partridge Stew

Donna, whose husband is a hunter, knows a thing or two about how to cook a partridge. Sometimes she will roast very young birds by rubbing them with butter, salt and pepper and baking them at 375° F for 25 to 30 minutes, or until tender.

Usually, though, she makes a partridge stew, which tenderizes the meat, no matter the age of the bird, and makes one partridge serve four people. The recipe sounds like any chicken stew, but the sweetness of the partridge meat gives it a difference you'll enjoy.

1 whole partridge breast
1 large onion, chopped
2 stalks celery, chopped
2 quarts water
2 carrots, sliced
2 large potatoes, peeled and chopped
1 cup rice
1 turnip, diced (optional)
Salt and pepper to taste

Simmer the partridge breast, onion and celery in the water for 1 hour, or until tender. Remove and reserve the partridge breast and add the carrots, potatoes, rice and the turnip, if you're using it, to the pot and simmer for another half hour or more, or until the rice is cooked and everything is tender. Chop and add the partridge meat. Season to taste with the salt and pepper.

• *SERVES 4.*

Fish

he many rivers and the tens of thousands of lakes in the Midwest yield tremendous quantities of freshwater fish. In addition, today, and for several decades back, lobsters are flown in and saltwater fish and shellfish of all sorts are widely available fresh, frozen or in cans. They're all put to good use.

Mount Pleasant Fried Catfish

If any catfish should come your way, here's what to do with them. As for me, every time I hear the word catfish, *I am almost overcome with one particular memory: My mother and I drove often from the East to Iowa. (Actually, she drove; I just complained.) It took two days to drive the 1300 miles (speed limits were different in those days). In the late afternoon of the second day, I kept watching for the roadside sign which would mean we were at last almost in Mount Pleasant. Finally, there it would be: "Eat at the Kit Kat Cafe, Home of the Catfish Sandwich." We were home!*

Not that any of us ever did eat at the Kit Kat Cafe. And, frankly, I am not a catfish fan. Most Midwesterners, though, think it's one of life's greatest pleasures. Here's the basic way to cook it, so I am told:

Dip cleaned and skinned small catfish or pieces of same first in milk, then in cornmeal. Fry, preferably in an inch or so of melted lard, turning once, until light brown. Sprinkle with salt and pepper to taste.

Pan-fried Perch or Trout with Brown-Butter Sauce

My grandfather, my mother, and Tom and "Bunny," my uncles on my mother's side, were all avid fishermen. The search for great fishing took them to many parts of North America (my grandfather even tried his luck north of the Arctic Circle when he was about eighty), but the most appreciated fish they ever caught were the local perch. These were cooked with gentle care, either by the side of the water over a wood fire or at home on the kitchen stove. A brown-butter sauce was the most elaboration anyone wanted, and often even that was omitted.

The same method can be used for trout, bluegills or other small fish or for pieces of larger fish.

4 whole brook trout, perch or other
    small fish, cleaned, or larger fish,
    cut into serving pieces
Flour for dredging
Salt and pepper
¼ cup fat for frying (see below)
4 tablespoons butter for the sauce

Give the fish a light coating of flour and sprinkle with salt and pepper.

The fat used to pan-fry the fish can be butter, bacon fat or oil. I come from a family of butter lovers, so that was our first choice, but some prefer other fats. Whatever you plan to use, heat it in a large frying pan and cook the fish, turning frequently, for about 8 minutes, or until it is light brown.

Remove the fish from the pan to a platter or plates. Pour off the fat in the pan. Replace it with 4 tablespoons of butter and cook till this turns a light nut-brown. Pour over the fish. • *SERVES 4.*

Wisconsin Fish Fry

If you're from Wisconsin, you've undoubtedly spent many Friday nights at the fish fries which are held all over the state at churches, fraternal organizations and restaurants. The menu is simple: fried perch, French fried potatoes and coleslaw. Add some pie, if that strikes your fancy, and you have a meal relished by the multitudes. Here's a cut-down version of how to fry the fish:

1 egg
¾ cup milk
½ teaspoon salt
4 fillets of perch
Flour for dredging
Fat for deep-frying

Beat the egg, then add the milk and salt to make a light batter. When you're ready to cook, heat the fat in a deep-fryer or kettle. Dip each fish fillet first into the batter, then into the flour. Give it a little shake, then put into the hot fat. (If you have a big enough fryer or kettle, you can cook all the fillets at once.) Fry until nicely brown on both sides. • *SERVES 4.*

Great Lakes Fish Boil

Wisconsin is home to another great fish event aside from the fish fry above. Door County, and Sturgeon Bay in particular, is the home of the famous Great Lakes Fish Boil. Mary Brittnacher of the Door County Library has sent me a fine description of this, and I pass it on to you, but must warn you not to try it at home quite the way they do it there (unless you have a fire truck standing by). I'm also giving you a home version, though.

Door County's inhabitants are mostly of Norwegian, English (via New England and New York), Irish, French-Canadian and German extraction. The fish boil, though, doesn't come from any of these heritages. Instead, it's a cooking method devised by Lake Michigan fishermen and now presented outdoors by many restaurants in the area during the summer months. Here's what happens:

A large wood fire is built outdoors. On this is placed a giant pot, tilted a bit to one side. Long pieces of firewood are placed vertically around the pot. Lake water is used (theoretically, at any rate) and it is heavily salted (I'll explain this in a minute).

When the water boils, a colanderlike basket filled with small onions and red new potatoes (with a small slice cut off the ends of each) is lowered into it. After about 25 minutes, another colander jammed with whitefish steaks goes into the water.

In about 7 minutes, everything is cooked, and now come the pyrotechnics. Some intrepid soul pours a bucket of kerosene onto the fire. Gigantic flames shoot up and the pot boils over on the side which is tipped down. The theory is that the heavy salting draws out any impurities in the water or the ingredients and that these are then disposed of as the water boils over.

Aside from the fish, potatoes, and onions, the feast consists of coleslaw, at least four kinds of bread (rye, date-nut, pumpkin and lemon), lots of melted butter and, for those able to eat more, cherry pie. Wisconsin beer is the traditional drink to go with a fish boil.

If you're determined to try a fish boil and can't get to Sturgeon Bay, you can come close by using regular tap water, lightly salted, in a pot on your kitchen stove or a charcoal grill outdoors. The most efficient pot to use is a spaghetti cooker or vegetable blancher, since it has a colanderlike insert. Cook the potatoes and onions for 25 minutes, then add the fish for about 7 minutes more. Lift out the pan's insert and serve. Forget the kerosene!

Baked Stuffed Pike or Other Large Fish

When the fisherman brings home a pike, whitefish, "muskie" or other large fish, it's often stuffed and baked, to the delight of almost everyone, but especially the cook, since there's practically no last-minute work to be done.

The stuffings vary as much as the ones for turkey. Every family has its favorite. Some prefer an all-vegetable filling (usually chopped onion, celery and tomatoes), but most like a simple bread-based stuffing such as this:

1 large (4 to 6 pound) pike or other large fish, cleaned
1 large onion, chopped
½ cup chopped celery
3 tablespoons butter
2 cups soft bread crumbs
¼ teaspoon poultry seasoning or thyme
Salt and pepper
1 egg, lightly beaten
2 tablespoons softened butter

Place the fish on buttered foil in a flat baking pan. Cook the onion and celery gently in the 3 tablespoons of butter for a few minutes, or until wilted but not brown. Add the bread crumbs, seasonings and egg and stuff the fish with the mixture, using skewers or thread to close the opening. Brush the softened butter over the top of the fish. Bake at 400° F for 40 minutes or more, depending on the size of the fish.
• *SERVES 6 to 8.*

Whole Fish Baked in Sour Cream and Onions

Here's one of the more glamorous Midwestern fish dishes, admired at many a dinner party.

1 4-pound freshwater fish, split, cleaned, boned and butterflied
Salt and pepper to taste
4 tablespoons butter, divided
1 medium onion, thinly sliced
2 cups sour cream
Chopped parsley for garnish

Rub the fish all over with salt, pepper and 2 tablespoons of the butter, softened. Put it, opened up flat skin side up, in a baking pan and broil, several inches away from the heat, until light brown.

Cook the onions in the rest of the butter until limp. Spread over the fish and top with the sour cream. Cover with foil and bake at 375° F for 25 minutes, or until thoroughly cooked. Sprinkle on the parsley.
• *SERVES 6 to 8.*

Fish Loaf

If luck's been good on the river or the lake, a Midwestern household can easily find itself with a glut of fish. A popular way to deal with this situation is to cook the fish, serve part of it then and save some to make a fish loaf in a day or two.

Even if it's not fishing season—or, heaven forbid, luck has not been with the angler—loaves are often made with canned salmon or tuna. In this case, use the juice in the can as part of the liquid needed for the loaf. The tuna casseroles containing canned soups and topped with crumbled corn flakes which came into use all over the country in the middle of the twentieth century probably evolved from fish loaves of this sort.

¾ cup soft bread crumbs
¼ cup minced onion
¼ cup minced green pepper
2 tablespoons minced parsley
   (optional)
1 egg, lightly beaten
½ cup milk
1 tablespoon melted butter
1 tablespoon lemon juice
Salt and pepper
2 cups cooked fish, flaked (any fish
   can be used—as can canned
   salmon or tuna)

Combine all the other ingredients, then gently fold in the fish. Put into a well-buttered small loaf pan and bake at 400° F for 30 minutes, or until firm.
• *SERVES 4.*

Pickled Fish

Pickled Fish was at first primarily made by the Norwegian settlers in Minnesota. However, it quickly spread to many other Midwestern areas. After all, this is a region of vinegar lovers.

1½ cups water (or more—see
   below)
1 teaspoon salt, divided
½ teaspoon ground black pepper,
   divided
¼ cup celery tops
1 pound freshwater fish, cleaned
   and cut into small pieces
1 small onion, sliced
½ cup cider vinegar
½ small hot red pepper
1½ teaspoons mixed pickling
   spices

Bring the water to a boil with ½ teaspoon salt, ¼ teaspoon black pepper and the celery tops. Meanwhile, bring another pot of water or a teakettle to a boil. Boil the seasoned water for 2 minutes, then add the fish. Now, if needed, add more boiling water until the fish is covered. Return to a boil; turn the heat down; cover; simmer for 5 minutes.

Remove the fish to a dish, using a slotted spoon. Combine the remaining salt and pepper with the onion, cider vinegar, hot pepper and pickling spices. Pour this over the fish. Refrigerate, covered, for 2 or 3 days, turning the fish carefully once a day. Serve cold.   • *SERVES 4.*

Lutefisk

Here is one dish you won't be able to make unless you live in certain parts of the Dakotas or Minnesota or other places with enough of a Scandinavian population to make it worthwhile for local stores to stock this delicacy, which is usually codfish, dried, then treated with such inedible chemicals as lye and sal soda. If you do live in one of these areas, you probably already know what to do with it. On the off chance that this isn't true, I'll sketch in how to proceed after you've bought your lutefisk *and brought it home.*

Wrap the *lutefisk* pieces in cheesecloth, then cook in gently simmering lightly salted water for about 10 minutes or until the fish flakes easily. Remove the bones and the skin (though some prefer to leave it on), then flake the fish or cut it into serving pieces.

For the simplest and most usual *lutefisk* dish, serve with mustard, boiled potatoes and an allspice-flavored white sauce.

Or dot the prepared *lutefisk* with butter and bake it at 300° F for 20 minutes.

Or make the following recipe, *Lutefisk* Pudding.

Lutefisk Pudding

Lutefisk lovers like this way the best.

1 cup uncooked rice
1 cup milk
1 cup water
Salt and pepper to taste
2 tablespoons butter, melted
2 eggs, beaten with 2 cups rich
  milk

Cook the rice in the milk and water. Place this in a casserole alternately with layers of flaked *lutefisk*. (Use about 1 pound.) Sprinkle each layer with a little salt, pepper and the melted butter. Finish with a layer of rice. Top with the egg-milk mixture. Bake at 325° F for about 1 hour.
• *SERVES 4.*

Midwestern Fish Pudding

Most Midwesterners don't have access to lutefisk (see above), but fish puddings of other sorts abound. This one is a typical example.

½ pound chopped or shredded
  raw fish
1 cup saltine crumbs
1 teaspoon salt
1½ cups light cream or rich milk
4 ounces melted butter
3 tablespoons minced parsley
6 egg whites, stiffly beaten

Combine the fish, saltine crumbs, salt and cream or milk in a bowl. Let it sit for 10 minutes to solidify a bit, then stir in the butter and parsley. Let sit for another 5 minutes, then fold in the stiffly beaten egg whites.

Put into a well-buttered casserole and bake at 325° F for 40 minutes, until set.
• *SERVES 4 to 6.*

Scalloped Oysters, Midwestern Style

Fresh oysters have been available in the Midwest for many years now, with the demand spurred by those who had spent time on the East Coast before moving on to greener pasturelands and now found themselves missing the inimitable oyster taste. Even in the nineteenth century, horse-drawn "oyster trains" reached as far as Ohio.

Some of these oysters were used in stews and in poultry dressings, and in the big cities, some were eaten raw, but most of them were scalloped. It's a dish I always associate with Midwestern Thanksgivings, where the feast will often include not only the traditional turkey but also country ham and scalloped oysters. While it's a little difficult to move after a meal of this sort, the combination of flavors and textures is wonderful.

The Midwestern touch is the hard-boiled eggs. Their original purpose was obviously to stretch the oysters, but they do make a good addition.

½ cup dry (but homemade) bread
  crumbs
1 cup cracker crumbs
½ cup melted butter
3 tablespoons light cream or rich
  milk
1 pint oysters, drained (but save
  their liquor)
Salt and pepper to taste
3 hard-boiled eggs, finely chopped

Combine the bread crumbs and cracker crumbs in a small bowl, then mix in the melted butter. In another bowl, or in a measuring cup, combine the cream or rich milk with 3 tablespoons of the liquor drained from the oysters and a little salt and pepper.

Now assemble your scallop: Sprinkle the bottom of a well-buttered baking dish with ⅓ of the buttered crumbs. Top with half the oysters, then pour on half the liquid. Next comes another layer of ⅓ of the crumbs, then the rest of the oysters, then the remaining crumbs and what's left of the liquid. Strew the chopped hard-boiled eggs across the top.

Bake at 400° F for 25 minutes.
• *SERVES 6.*

Shrimp Wiggle

Just the name alone is enough to ensure this dish a spot in the Midwestern recipe hall of fame. Fortunately, it tastes delicious, too. In the days when Chicken à la King, served in a patty shell, was the all-too-standard fare served on ceremonial occasions, Shrimp Wiggle made a pleasant change. It was also cooked in many a chafing dish as a show-off dish. Today's cooks are more apt to make their Shrimp Wiggle in the kitchen and serve it on toast.

The essential, unvarying ingredients of Shrimp Wiggle are shrimp, cream sauce and peas. After that, most cooks add a little something of their own. Some of these "little somethings" are listed below.

4 tablespoons butter
2 tablespoons flour
1½ cups milk
Salt and pepper to taste
1 cup or more small shrimp, cooked, peeled and deveined
½ cup peas, cooked (or frozen peas, thawed)

POSSIBLE ADDITIONS

Lemon juice or sherry (a teaspoon or 2 added to the cream sauce)
Sliced olives or diced celery (mixed into the sauce), chopped toasted almonds, chopped parsley or paprika (sprinkled onto the dish)

Make a cream sauce by melting the butter, stirring in the flour, cooking and stirring for 3 to 4 minutes, then adding the milk and stirring or whisking over medium-low heat until the sauce thickens and comes to a boil. Add the salt and pepper and any other seasonings you wish to use, then stir in the shrimp and peas.

Heat gently, then serve in heated pastry shells or on freshly made buttered toast.
• *SERVES 4.*

Shrimp de Jonghe

This continental-sounding and quite elegant dish originated in a Chicago restaurant circa 1900. It was very popular in the Midwest and elsewhere for quite a while. Then, like most food fads, it was forgotten. Since it's one of the best of all ways to serve shrimp, it really should be brought back into favor.

2 pounds shrimp, cooked, peeled and deveined
6 tablespoons butter, at room temperature
¼ teaspoon minced or pressed garlic
2 tablespoons finely minced parsley
¼ teaspoon paprika
A dash of cayenne
Salt and pepper to taste
½ cup fine, dry bread crumbs (preferably homemade)
¼ cup dry sherry

Arrange the shrimp in 4 shallow, well-buttered individual baking dishes or 1 large dish.

Mix the butter with the garlic, parsley, paprika, cayenne and salt and pepper, then stir in the bread crumbs and sherry. Top the shrimp with this mixture. Bake at 375° F for 30 minutes, or until the bread crumbs are light brown. • *SERVES 4.*

Clam Fritters

Clams in the shell do turn up in their markets, but most Midwesterners keep to their old traditions of using canned minced clams in various dishes. One of the best and most loved of these is this delectable morsel, the clam fritter.

2 6½-ounce cans minced clams (about 1 cup after draining)
2 eggs, lightly beaten
⅓ cup juice from the clams
⅓ cup milk
1⅓ cups flour
2 teaspoons baking powder
¼ teaspoon paprika
Salt and pepper
¼ cup minced onion
Bacon grease or other fat

Drain the clams, saving the juice. Mix the eggs with the clam juice and milk in a bowl. Combine the flour, baking powder, paprika and salt and pepper and stir into the egg mixture. Next, stir in the clams and onion.

Heat 2 or 3 tablespoons of whatever fat you want to use over fairly high heat in a large frying pan. (Bacon grease will give the most flavor.) Drop the clam mixture into this in large spoonfuls and fry until puffed and crisp and brown on both sides. (You may need to add more fat as you go.) Drain on paper towels—or be very Midwestern and use cut-up brown grocery bags.
• *MAKES 12 to 14 big fritters, serving 4 to 6.*

Most Midwestern kitchens contain a can with a carefully acquired cache of bacon fat. For these fritters, though, many people cook fresh bacon to serve along with the dish. Clams and bacon are a natural combination.

Clam and Corn Fritters

Here's a small variation to placate those who feel all fritters should contain some corn. There are those who like maple syrup with this sort of fritter; I'm one of them.

Just add ½ cup cooked corn kernels to the batter for Clam Fritters. Cook and drain exactly as you would the regular Clam Fritters. Serve with maple syrup if it appeals to you.

Cold Lobster Mousse

Don't think for a moment that there are no lobsters in the Midwest. There are lots of them—they fly them in, and have been doing so for many years. We used to go over to the Elks Club in Fairfield, Iowa, for dinner once or twice a month. Nobody in the family was an Elk, but that didn't matter at all; the restaurant was open to the public. It had two enticing attractions.

First, liquor was served there, a rarity at that time in southeastern Iowa. I've mentioned elsewhere my grandfather's strong feelings against liquor. These prejudices were not shared by his children, though no one ever dared drink in front of him. We tended to go over to the Elks Club on the nights he attended his Rotary Club meetings. I wonder if he ever knew why.

Second, and I do think more importantly, the Elks had the gumption to fly live lobsters in from the East Coast. That was exciting!

In the big cities, lobster was more of an everyday occurrence. So unless canned lobster was used, dishes such as this scrumptious summer main dish were mainly confined to Chicago, Detroit and other such centers of population.

1 tablespoon (1 packet) plain
   gelatine
¼ cup cold water
Minced lobster—the meat of a
   2-pound cooked lobster or
   1½ cups of canned lobster meat
½ cup minced celery
½ cup minced apple
⅔ cup mayonnaise
2 tablespoons lemon juice
Salt and cayenne pepper to taste
½ cup heavy cream, whipped

Combine the gelatine and cold water in the top of a double boiler over boiling water and stir until dissolved, about 5 minutes. Cool a bit, then mix in the remaining ingredients, ending with the whipped cream. Pour into a 2-quart mold that has first been rinsed in water (this will make unmolding easier). Chill for at least 2 hours, or until firm. • SERVES 6.

Sunday

Night

Suppers

*I*n this chapter, you'll find a lot of the very best food from the heartland. These are the dishes served on Sunday night, if you've had a big noontime Sunday dinner, or at any other time (lunch, for instance) when you might want a light meal. Many of them are also what you might take to a covered-dish or potluck supper. In the days when most families had their big meal in the middle of the day, every night was supper night.

Some recipes in other sections of this book might well turn up for Sunday night supper, too—any of the soups, for instance, especially when accompanied by homemade hot breads. Lots of families have a tradition of pancakes for Sunday suppers, and waffles show up then, too, often topped with such salubrious mixtures as Creamed Chicken and Ham (see page 83). And then there are some people who would prefer to eat a meal of this sort every single night of the year, whether or not they've had a big meal at lunchtime.

Slumgullion

There are a lot of macaroni and ground beef dishes in the heartland, but none of them, in my highly prejudiced opinion, can compare with my grandmother's version, Slumgullion. The cheese in Slumgullion makes the difference, I think, and the fact that the macaroni cooks right along with the other ingredients, absorbing all that good flavor. It has a sharpness and distinction lacking in most other such dishes.

1 pound ground beef
1 teaspoon butter
¼ cup minced onion
¼ cup minced green pepper
1 cup tomato sauce
1 cup uncooked elbow macaroni
Salt and pepper to taste
2 tablespoons Parmesan cheese

Brown the ground beef with the butter in a big frying pan. Add the onion and green pepper and cook for 2 to 3 minutes more, then add the tomato sauce and macaroni and enough water to cover—about 2 cups. Simmer for approximately 15 minutes, stirring occasionally and adding more water if needed. Season with salt and pepper. Stir in the Parmesan cheese at the very last.
• *SERVES 4 to 6.*

This is a flexible dish. You can leave out the green pepper, add celery or carrots, use fresh or canned tomatoes instead of sauce, use different pasta shapes, etc. Do what you want with it, as long as you use ground meat, pasta, onions, cheese and some sort of tomato. Herbs would not feel at home in Slumgullion, though.

Helen's Iowa Dish

My friend Helen Hackett Kelly learned how to cook this casserole when she was a freshman at the University of Iowa and has been making it ever since with much regularity. She has always called it her "Iowa dish." She's cooked it for me, and it's really good. It's also simple to assemble and, like so many other Midwestern dishes, reliable.

1 medium onion, minced
1 clove garlic, minced or pressed
1 tablespoon butter or bacon fat
1 pound ground beef
1 1-pound can tomatoes
1 1-pound can kidney beans
1 cup raw white rice
Salt, pepper and chili powder to taste

Brown the onion and garlic in the butter or bacon fat in a large frying pan, then add the ground beef and cook over medium heat until, in the words of Helen's recipe, "crumbly." Stir in the tomatoes and kidney beans (both undrained) and the rice. Add salt, pepper and chili powder to taste. Put into a buttered casserole and bake, covered at 300° F for 1 hour and 40 minutes, then remove the cover and bake 20 minutes more. • *SERVES 4 to 6.*

Scalloped Sausage Meat and Potatoes

The "scallop" (or sometimes "escallop") is a way of cooking very popular in the Midwest—not that anyone, including me, has a very strong idea what it means to "scallop" something. I have a hazy concept that a scallop is almost anything that is cooked in a baking dish, saturated with milk and browned on top. The original scalloped dish is probably Scalloped Potatoes (page 109), but Scalloped Sausage Meat and Potatoes makes a fine supper dish.

1 pound sausage meat
4 medium potatoes, peeled and thinly sliced
1 medium onion, thinly sliced
Salt and pepper
A little flour
About 2 cups milk (see below)

Cook the sausage meat briefly, breaking it up, until it loses its color and some of the fat oozes out. Now assemble the scallop: Grease a 9 × 12-inch casserole or gratin dish with some of the sausage fat or with butter. Put in layers of potatoes, onions and sausage meat, sprinkling each layer with a little salt, pepper and flour and ending with a layer of potatoes on top. Add milk until it is clearly visible under the top layer—in the dish I use, this takes about 2 cups of milk. Cover. Bake at 375° F for 40 minutes, then remove the cover and bake 20 minutes more, or until the top is brownish.
• *SERVES 4.*

Sausage Baked with Pineapple

This is one of those natural, but not often encountered, flavor combinations that really work. It goes especially well with sweet potatoes baked in their skins.

8 slices pineapple
2 tablespoons mustard (for instance, the country mustard on page 203)
1 pound sausage meat
4 tablespoons minced chives or parsley

Put the pineapple slices in a baking pan. Pat them dry, then spread with the mustard. Make the sausage meat into 8 large, flat patties and put one on each slice of pineapple. Bake at 350° F for 35 minutes, or until the pineapple has begun to brown and caramelize a bit. Serve sprinkled with the chives or parsley. • *SERVES 4.*

Sausage Scrapple

The Pennsylvania Dutch and the Philadelphians, who claim scrapple, a highly seasoned meat dish, as their own, would probably be horrified at this recipe. Their version is made from many parts of the pig (usually unavailable except to those who slaughter their own), and it certainly doesn't contain tomato juice.

But this Midwestern scrapple is just as

good as theirs, and a great deal simpler, since all the meat chopping and almost all the seasoning has been done for you by the sausage makers.

3 cups water
¼ cup tomato juice
1 cup yellow cornmeal
1 teaspoon poultry seasoning
½ pound sausage meat, cooked until any pink color is gone
1 lightly beaten egg
Cracker crumbs
Butter or other fat for frying at the end

Bring the water and tomato juice to a boil in a fairly large saucepan, then turn the heat down so the liquid is just simmering. Sprinkle the cornmeal in very slowly, in a thin stream, stirring constantly. Continue to cook and stir for 15 to 20 minutes, or until very stiff. (If you have a microwave oven, this would be a handy place to use it. See below.)

Now add the poultry seasoning and sausage meat to the cornmeal mixture. Mix well (a food processor helps here), then pack into a loaf pan and chill thoroughly (overnight, at least).

To serve, cut the scrapple into 1-inch slices. Dip the slices first in the beaten egg, then in the cracker crumbs, and fry slowly in batches in a large frying pan in a small amount of butter or other fat until both sides are brown and crisp.
• *SERVES 4 to 6.*

MICROWAVE VARIATION
Combine the cornmeal, water and tomato juice in a 2-quart glass measuring cup. Mi-

crowave on High for 6 minutes. Stir well, then microwave on High for another 6 minutes. (Total time: 12 minutes. Total work: very little.) Then continue with the recipe as above.

Goette

My daughter Candace, who's now living there, ferreted out this special treat of the Cincinnati area for me. There's a large German population in Cincinnati, and this is one of their most beloved dishes. You can buy it in grocery stores there, packaged in little plastic-wrapped rolls that look like sausage meat. Or you can make your own. It's like a cross between sausage and scrapple (with oatmeal replacing the cornmeal) and so good that more of the world should know about it. It's easy to make, too, though time-consuming. Pronouncing it's the hard part. If you can say the name of Goethe, the great German poet, you've got it. Otherwise, try "Gheutuh" or "Getta," as in "get a horse."

2 quarts water
2 pounds lean pork, cut in 1-inch cubes
1 medium onion, chopped coarsely
2⅔ cups uncooked oatmeal
½ teaspoon salt
⅛ teaspoon pepper
½ cup flour (optional)
Butter or other fat for frying

Bring the water to a boil. Add the pork and onion and simmer until tender (about half an hour.) Remove the pork and onion and grind them fine in a meat grinder (or use a food processor). Bring the broth the pork has cooked in back to a boil and slowly trickle in the oatmeal, stirring, adding more water if necessary. Add the ground pork, onion and the salt and pepper and simmer for 45 minutes, stirring frequently and checking to see if you need to add more water to prevent the mixture from sticking to the pan.

Cool slightly, then either pack into a loaf pan or form into a roll and wrap securely in foil or plastic wrap. Chill well. When ready to eat your Goette, cut it into about ¾-inch-thick slices. Dip it on both sides in the flour, if you wish. (Some do, some don't.) Cook in a little hot butter or other fat until brown on both sides.

• *SERVES 6 to 8.*

Very Special Macaroni and Cheese

As I've said elsewhere, most Midwestern-ers are far from extravagant in their approach to all aspects of life, including cooking. This is definitely not to say, though, that they are stingy. Especially in food, they go for the best available, and they aren't tightfisted with it.

When you look at this recipe, you may think that the layer of tomatoes is what makes it "very special." Not so. What makes it stand out in the crowd of other such dishes is the large amount of good cheese. As my grandmother's generation used to say, "If a thing's worth doing at all, it's worth doing right." So if you're making macaroni and cheese, throw the cheese in with a wild and liberal hand.

3 tablespoons butter
3 tablespoons flour
1½ cups rich milk
Salt and pepper to taste
2 dashes hot pepper sauce
2 cups (½ pound) grated or
  shredded sharp Cheddar cheese
8 ounces elbow macaroni, cooked
  until barely tender
1 large tomato, sliced

Melt the butter in a fairly large saucepan. Add the flour and cook and stir for 3 to 4 minutes. Add the milk all at once and stir until the sauce comes to a boil and thickens. Mix in the seasonings, then the cheese, and continue to cook over low heat, still stirring, until the cheese has melted. Stir in the cooked macaroni. Put half this mixture in a well-buttered 2-quart baking dish. Top first with the tomato slices, then the rest of the macaroni and sauce. Bake at 350° F for 30 minutes, or until brown on top, the way a good macaroni and cheese is supposed to be. • *SERVES 4 to 6.*

Noodle and Cottage Cheese Casserole

This recipe reminds me of the potluck lunches that were held once a week at the Mount Pleasant Country Club. The country club had a short golf course, though I don't recall ever seeing anyone actually play on it. The main outdoor sport there was cutthroat croquet, played on courts framed with wooden edges to permit tricky ricochet shots. Then, on the Fourth of July, after family picnics, the children raced around, acquiring grass stains on our clothes, until darkness came and with it, fireworks.

At the lunches, the ladies whose last name began with letters A to N brought the food one week, those from M to Z the next. You might expect some of the ladies to cheat by attending only on the weeks they weren't expected to bring food, but if anything, it was just the opposite. These were women who were proud of their cooking and happy to show it off. (The only scandal was occasioned by one young woman, new to the community, who went down the long food-laden table, not only filling her plate amply but also quietly— but not unobserved—stuffing homemade rolls and cookies into the umbrella she was carrying. No one could figure this out, since she and her husband did not lack for money. Perhaps, everyone decided, it was cooking skills she was short on. From then on, kindly ladies offered her recipes whenever they saw her.)

8 ounces medium noodles, cooked
2 cups small-curd cottage cheese
1/4 cup minced scallions
2 tablespoons minced parsley
2 cups sour cream, divided
1/4 cup grated Parmesan cheese

Combine the noodles with the cottage cheese, scallions, parsley and 1½ cups of the sour cream. Place in a low, buttered casserole. Spread on the remaining ½ cup of sour cream and sprinkle on the Parmesan cheese. Bake at 350° F for 45 minutes or until the top is light brown.
• *SERVES 6.*

Creamed Chicken and Ham on Waffles

When my father became nostalgic for his boyhood days in Kansas City, Missouri, sometimes he would sing his old high school song, "Fairfield High, we dearly love thee." At other times, he would talk about the food he especially enjoyed in those days. Inevitably, he mentioned Creamed Chicken and Ham on Waffles.

The lemon juice added at the end is my idea. To me, it gives this dish a little needed zip. I doubt if my grandmother Ellis used it—especially since citrus fruits were so hard to come by and expensive in those days.

FOR THE CREAM SAUCE

4 tablespoons butter, divided
3 tablespoons flour
1 cup chicken broth
1 cup rich milk or light cream
Salt and pepper to taste (be cautious with the salt—the ham contains a lot of it)
1 teaspoon lemon juice

2 cups diced cooked chicken
½ cup diced cooked ham
4 to 6 large waffles (see page 153)

Make a cream sauce: Melt 3 tablespoons of the butter and stir in the flour. Cook and stir for 3 to 4 minutes, then add the broth and milk or cream all at once. Combine well, then simmer, stirring, until the sauce bubbles and thickens. Season to taste, then stir in the lemon juice and the last tablespoon of butter.

Combine the chicken and ham with the sauce and heat very gently. Serve over freshly made waffles. • *SERVES 4 to 6.*

Cornish Pasties

Unless you're one of them, you may not know of the sizable number of emigrants from Cornwall to be found in the states of Michigan and Wisconsin. My friend Jan Saundry married into one of these families and learned how to make Cornish Pasties from her mother-in-law. Jan not only told me about the great pasties of Michigan but also taught me how to pronounce the name: past *as in "the long-ago past," not* paste *as in library.*

These are wonderful little meat turnovers, originally designed to be taken to work with them by Cornish miners, and they're about the most portable food you can imagine. You can make them with a regular piecrust dough, but they won't have the extraordinary sturdiness given by this suet crust.

FOR THE PASTRY DOUGH

3 cups flour
½ teaspoon salt
1½ cups ground or finely chopped beef suet
2 tablespoons lard
About ½ cup cold water

1 pound raw round steak, finely diced or minced
½ pound raw pork, finely diced or minced
1 medium potato, peeled and minced
¾ cup minced onion
1 small turnip or carrot, peeled and minced
1 teaspoon salt
¼ teaspoon pepper

Make a pastry dough from the first 5 ingredients: Combine the flour and salt. Cut in the suet and lard. Add enough cold water to make a slightly moist dough. (A food processor makes all this very easy.) Chill.

Now make the filling by combining all the other ingredients.

Divide the dough into 8 parts. Roll each into a 6½- to 7-inch circle. Put approximately ¼ cup of filling in the middle of each circle, then bring 2 sides of the pastry circle to the top around the filling and crimp the edges together with your fingers. Place on a flat pan and bake at 400° F for 50 minutes to 1 hour, or until light brown.

Cornish pasties are good hot, cold or at any stage in between. They can be kept warm—or frozen and reheated. • *MAKES 8.*

Meat Pies of the Germans from Russia

Another group you may not know of, the "Germans from Russia," make a specialty of this sort of meat pie. Back in the 1700s, Russia, under Catherine the Great, lured 100,000 Germans to settle and farm there by offers of exemption from taxes and from military service. About 100 years later, the exemptions were withdrawn, and the Germans were pressured to leave.

Some returned to Germany, but a large number came to live in the American Midwest, in a strip which included the Dakotas, Kansas, Nebraska and Oklahoma. Their language and religion (Lutheran or Mennonite) were intact, and their food remained primarily German. The filling for their meat pies is reminiscent of one used in Russian piroshki, though, so perhaps there's evidence here of their hundred-year sojourn under the czars.

½ recipe for Light, Delicious Yeast
   Roll Dough (page 141), using only
   1 teaspoon sugar

FOR THE FILLING

¾ pound lean ground beef
1 medium onion, minced
1 teaspoon butter
½ cup beef broth or water
Salt and pepper to taste

While the dough is rising, prepare the filling: Brown the beef and onion in the butter over medium-high heat, stirring to break up any clumps of meat, then turn down the heat, add the broth or water and the salt and pepper and simmer until the liquid has disappeared. Allow to cool.

Now divide the dough into 4 equal parts. One at a time, roll each into roughly an 8½ × 7-inch rectangle. Top each with ¼ of the meat mixture, leaving a border all around. Fold, envelope-fashion, by bringing one long edge down, then folding in the end pieces, then bringing up the other long edge. Seal the seams by pinching. Place on a baking sheet, seam side down, cover and allow to rise for half an hour. Bake at 375° F for 15 minutes, or until brown.
• *MAKES 4.*

Italian Spaghetti, Midwestern Style

It's a long way from Italy to the Midwest, a fact clearly evident when you look at most pasta recipes from the heartland. This one, from my family's friend Nona Spahr Donahue, is more authentic than most (it even tells you not to break the spaghetti before cooking) and makes a marvelous supper dish.

¾ cup chopped parsley
¾ cup chopped onions
¾ cup chopped celery leaves
2 tablespoons bacon fat
2 cloves garlic, pressed
¾ pound lamb, cut in very small
  cubes
¾ pound veal, cut in very small
  cubes
2 teaspoons black pepper
Salt to taste
12 ounces (2 small cans) Italian-
  flavored tomato paste
12 ounces water (use the tomato
  paste cans to measure)
1½ pounds spaghetti (do not
  break)
Grated Parmesan cheese

Cook the parsley, onions and celery leaves in the bacon fat until, in Nona's words, "the parsley curls up." Add the garlic, lamb and veal and keep cooking until the meats are well browned. Now add the black pepper and salt, the tomato paste and water. Simmer gently for 1 hour, adding a little more water if needed.

Nona's recipe says to cook the spaghetti and mix it with the sauce, but you might prefer to serve the sauce on top. At any rate, pass some grated Parmesan for everyone to sprinkle on to taste. • *SERVES 6 TO 8.*

Nona said to get the meat from lamb and veal chops. If this seems too wildly extravagant, use stewing meat, cooking the dish a little longer. Also, you could use beef or pork if you wish.

Toasted Ravioli

Whoever heard of Toasted Ravioli? Hardly anyone except for those who live in and around St. Louis, Missouri. It's a local specialty and tremendously popular. When you try it, you'll see why.

You'll find a simpler but not quite as popular variation, Fried Ravioli, at the end of the recipe.

18 ravioli (see below)
Flour for dredging
Milk for dipping
Dry bread crumbs for coating
Oil for deep frying, heated to
   375° F on a deep-fry thermometer
Grated Parmesan cheese for
   sprinkling (optional)
Sauce for serving (see below)

The ravioli can be homemade or store-bought, frozen or not, and they can be any flavor you want. I prefer cheese ravioli, but that's just me. (And I am not the world's greatest ravioli fan—unless they're toasted or fried.)

Dip the ravioli on both sides in the flour. (If they're homemade ravioli, already coated with a dusting of flour, you can skip this step.) Then dip the ravioli on both sides into the milk, then the bread crumbs.

Now fry them, a few a time, in a deep fat fryer or wok until golden, turning from time to time. (This frying of the breaded ravioli is the "toasting.") Remove to paper towels and, if you want to use the cheese, sprinkle it on right away. Allow to cool a bit before serving. Some like these ravioli with an Italian meat sauce or a plainer tomato sauce. Others including me, think melted butter is sufficient. • *SERVES 4.*

FRIED RAVIOLI
Flour the ravioli and fry in the deep fat as above. Skip the breading, but add the sprinkling of grated cheese and the sauce, if you so desire.

Nebraska Baked Beans

It's hard to pin down the origin of baked beans, but it is known that dry beans had been used for a long time by the Native Americans. The New England, or Boston, version has traditionally included salt pork and some sort of sweetening, usually molasses or maple syrup, and sometimes onion and a bit of dry mustard.

The baked beans of the Midwest probably began with the early settlers from the East. New Englanders whose ancestors stayed put on the East Coast still stick rather closely to the recipe of their forebears, but in typical heartland fashion, the adventurous Midwestern pioneers and their descendants began adding whatever struck their fancy to the dish. I have seen Midwestern baked bean recipes which call for everything from chili sauce to Worcestershire sauce to coffee to chopped pickles. This Nebraska version is more restrained than some, and it is lovely. (The apples and vinegar make a big difference.)

1 pound small dry white beans
5 cups water (plus more for soaking)
½ teaspoon dry mustard
1 tablespoon cider vinegar
¼ pound salt pork, skinned, coarsely diced
½ cup diced onion
2 apples, peeled and chopped
¼ cup unsulphured molasses
1 teaspoon salt

Soak the beans overnight in enough water to cover by several inches, then drain. Put the beans in a large pot with 5 cups of fresh water and simmer for 1 hour, or until tender.

Combine the dry mustard with the cider vinegar and add to the beans along with all the other ingredients. Put into a deep covered casserole or, preferably, a bean pot. Bake at 300° F for 5 hours, covered, then check to see if you need to add more water. Bake for another hour, uncovered, to brown the top. • *SERVES 4 to 6.*

Swedish Baked Omelette

Give me any tart jelly, some freshly made dinner rolls and a liberal helping of Swedish Baked Omelette, puffed, brown and quivering, for a Sunday night supper and I feel the world is treating me well.

½ pound bacon, cut into small
  pieces
5 eggs
3 tablespoons flour
2 cups milk
Salt and pepper to taste
A pinch of allspice

Cook the bacon until crisp in an ovenproof frying pan. Beat the eggs thoroughly (I use a blender), then beat in first the flour, then the milk and seasonings. Reheat the bacon, pour off all but about 3 tablespoons of the fat, and pour on the egg mixture. Bake at 375° F for about half an hour, or until lightly browned. Wherever it's available, this is served with Lingonberry preserves, but cranberry sauce or tart jellies are often substituted, and some serve it with seedless black raspberry jam. • *SERVES 2 to 4.*

Eggs in a Nest

Cozy is the first adjective that comes to mind when I think of Midwestern Eggs in a Nest. Others apply, though—good-tasting, always enjoyed and savory, for instance.

3 cups mashed potatoes (pages
  112 to 113)
Hot milk (optional—see below)
4 tablespoons minced scallions
4 tablespoons butter, divided
¾ cup finely minced ham or crisp,
  crumbled bacon
Salt and pepper to taste
6 eggs

Soften the mashed potatoes with a little hot milk if they've been made ahead and have stiffened. Cook the scallions gently in 2 tablespoons of the butter until softened and add to the mashed potatoes along with the ham or bacon and salt and pepper to taste.

Put into a baking pan and make 6 large depressions in the potatoes with the back of a spoon. Break an egg into each depression. Melt the remaining 2 tablespoons of butter and drizzle it over the dish. Bake at 350° F for 10 minutes or a bit more, watching to make sure the eggs are set but not hard. • *SERVES 3 to 6.*

Spinach and Cheese Fondue

Here's another example of an American fondue, this one glistening with spinach and onions. It's a pretty dish to look at and makes an ideal supper, especially when accompanied by tomatoes in some form.

    7 slices white bread
    3 tablespoons butter, at room
       temperature
    3 eggs
    1½ cups milk
    1 pound spinach, cooked and
       chopped (or 1 10-ounce
       package frozen chopped
       spinach, thawed and drained)
    2 tablespoons minced onion
    1 cup grated Cheddar cheese
    1 tablespoon lemon juice
    A dash of ground cayenne pepper
       or Tabasco sauce
    Salt and pepper

Remove the crusts from the bread, then spread with the butter. Put 4 of the slices in the bottom of a large round baking dish or frying pan (a 12-inch iron skillet is ideal). Cut the other 3 slices into 3 strips each and put aside for the moment.

Blend or beat the eggs and milk together and pour ½ cup of the mixture onto the pieces of bread in the dish. Set the rest aside.

Now combine the spinach, onion, cheese, lemon juice, cayenne or Tabasco and salt and pepper and spread over the 4 pieces of bread. Put the 9 strips of bread on as though they were the spokes of a wheel, then pour on the rest of the egg-milk mixture. Let the dish sit for at least half an hour, then bake at 350° F for 50 to 60 minutes, or until the spokes of bread have puffed and browned. • *SERVES 4.*

Savory American Fondue

In much of the heartland, dishes of this sort appear frequently. They're a far cry from the fondues of Switzerland, those convivial pots of melted cheese and wine served with French bread for dunking, but they're just as nice in their own way. (If you want a real Swiss fondue, go to New Glarus, Wisconsin.) Some call their version of this sort of thing a cheese pudding, and an apt name it is for this casseroleful of goodness. The top browns, the bottom forms a sort of crust and the middle is full of a soft mixture of cheese, bread, eggs and milk, with just a slight tang of mustard.

6 slices white or whole wheat bread
4 tablespoons butter, at room
   temperature
1 tablespoon prepared mustard
3 eggs
2¼ cups milk
¾ pound cheddar cheese, cut in
   1-inch cubes or grated
Salt and pepper

Spread the bread with a mixture of the butter and mustard. Cut each slice of bread into squares (make 2 cuts across and 2 up and down and you'll have 9 squares per piece of bread). Put into a buttered casserole. Put the rest of the ingredients in a blender or food processor. Whir until the mixture is amalgamated, then pour onto the bread cubes. Bake at 350° F for half an hour. • *SERVES 4 to 6.*

Mrs. Thompson's Festive Egg Casserole

This recipe comes from Mrs. James R. Thompson, the wife of the former governor of Illinois. Her title is apt—this is indeed a festive dish.

1½ cups grated Cheddar cheese
½ cup grated Swiss cheese
½ cup grated mozzarella cheese
2 tablespoons minced green
   pepper
2 tablespoons minced onion
½ pound mushrooms, sliced and
   sautéed in 3 tablespoons butter
   (Mrs. Thompson suggests 1 6-
   ounce can mushrooms, drained
   and sliced)
¾ cup crumbled cooked bacon or
   sausage
8 eggs
½ cup milk

Combine the 3 cheeses. Put half of this mixture in the bottom of a well-buttered 9 × 13-inch pan. Top first with the green pepper, onion, mushrooms and the bacon or sausage, then with the rest of the cheese. Beat the eggs and milk together lightly and pour over the casserole. Bake, covered, at 400° F for 30 minutes.
• *SERVES 8 to 10.*

Little Switzerland Cheese Pie

When you go to New Glarus, Wisconsin, you step off from mid-America to the heart of Switzerland. New Glarus, sometimes called Little Switzerland, was established in 1850 by immigrants from the Swiss canton of Glarus. The first settlers tried to farm the land, but since they had not been farmers at home, this did not go well. A cheese-making venture was then begun, and it prospered.

Today's descendants of the Swiss settlers have clung to their old ways, even in some cases speaking a dialect which has since died out in Switzerland itself. The architecture there is Swiss-inspired, they make Swiss embroideries, they eat Swiss food—and they sell the embroideries and other crafts and the food to hordes of tourists who want to experience a quick trip to a foreign ambience. You'll find a museum, a historical Swiss village, yodeling demonstrations, a William Tell festival and a number of Swiss shops and restaurants there. New Glarus is fun!

I'm indebted to Doris Streiff, author of Down on the Farm *and a Swiss-descendant* resident of New Glarus, for the recipe for this Swiss cheese pie. (Its Swiss name is Kaesekuchen.) To read the recipe, you'd expect a quiche of the French sort, but it's quite different, since the emphasis is on the cheese and onions, not the custard. It's a real cheese pie, and delicious.

¾ pound natural Swiss cheese, grated
1 tablespoon flour
1 9-inch deep-dish piecrust (see page 162)
2 medium onions, finely chopped
3 tablespoons butter
1 cup milk
3 eggs, beaten
Salt and pepper to taste
¼ teaspoon nutmeg

Toss the cheese with the flour and put half of it in the piecrust. Cook the onions in the butter until light brown and spread over the cheese in the crust. Top with the other half of the cheese. Now combine the milk, eggs, salt and pepper. Pour over the cheese and onions. Sprinkle on the nutmeg.

Bake at 400° F for 15 minutes, then reduce to 300° F and bake for another 30 minutes, or until a knife inserted in the center comes out clean. • *SERVES 4 as a main dish.*

Spanish Rice

As far as I know, this recipe has no direct link with Spain. The words Spanish or Creole, *which turn up frequently on heartland menus, imply that a dish contains tomatoes, onions and often green peppers.*

This passes (and very nicely, too) for a main dish at supper, though it would only rank as a side dish if served as part of a dinner.

½ cup chopped bacon
½ cup chopped onion
¼ cup finely chopped green
  pepper
2 cups cooked rice
3 cups tomatoes, peeled, seeded
  and chopped (or canned)
2 teaspoons sugar
½ teaspoon salt

Cook the bacon in a large frying pan until it begins to brown, then add the onion and green pepper and cook for 5 minutes. Now stir in the rest of the ingredients and cook gently for another 5 minutes. Spoon into a buttered casserole dish and bake at 350° F.
• *SERVES 4 to 6.*

Janson's Temptation

Janson's Temptation is a potato fantasy that is usually served as a main course for supper. You'll find it in Sweden, where it's very popular, but there's an interesting legend, which I haven't been able to substantiate but choose to believe, that the dish reversed the usual homeland-to-heartland route and was invented in Illinois, then sent back to the old country in letters from the settlers to those they had left behind.

The legend claims that Janson was a minister who, after one taste of this dish, totally abandoned (temporarily, we hope) his vows of asceticism. One taste of it might do the same to you.

2 pounds potatoes, peeled and cut
  into ¼-inch French fry shapes
1½ cups thinly sliced onions
1 3½-ounce tin anchovy fillets
Pepper
1½ cups light cream (or a little
  more)
2 tablespoons butter

Place half the pieces of potato in a well-buttered 2-quart baking dish. Top with the onions and anchovies and the rest of the potatoes, then sprinkle on a little pepper. Pour on the light cream. (If there's not enough cream to cover the potatoes, use a bit more.) Dot the top with small pieces of the butter. Bake at 375° F for 45 to 50 minutes, or until tender. • *SERVES 4.*

Hot Supper Sandwiches

Hot supper sandwiches come in a number of varieties—turkey, chicken, roast beef, and so on. It all depends on what you have on hand, usually the remnants of a roast from Sunday dinner. There are those who prefer the hot sandwich to the original presentation, possibly because it doesn't have as many side dishes accompanying it, but also because of a widespread love of bread saturated with hot gravy.

You don't really need a formal recipe to make a basic hot supper sandwich. The main thing to know is that you use just bread, not toast, as the base, and only 1 slice per sandwich. Put a slice of bread on each plate; top with warmed-up slices of turkey or whatever, then liberally cover with hot gravy. In the case of turkey, be sure to put a little cranberry sauce on the plate. Pickled Peaches (see page 195) go well with any hot sandwich, too.

Reuben Sandwiches

All my life, I've assumed, without giving it much thought, that the Reuben sandwich was a New York City invention. After all, there was a famous restaurant there by that name, and the ingredients seem to be typical New York deli fare.

Now I've read that the Reuben was invented in Nebraska in the 1920s by a man named Reuben Kay and is yet another example of Midwestern ingenuity when it comes to food. I've also read substantiation of the New York theory. Either way, it makes a perfect supper dish and is greatly admired in the Midwest.

FOR EACH SANDWICH

2 slices rye bread
3 tablespoons Thousand Island dressing
2 slices Swiss cheese
1 ½ tablespoons sauerkraut
2 slices cooked corned beef
1 ½ tablespoons soft butter

Spread the bread slices on one side with the dressing, then stack up the cheese, sauerkraut and corned beef, forming a closed sandwich. Spread the soft butter on the outside of the sandwich and cook on a grill until both sides are brown and the cheese has melted. Cut into 3 diagonal pieces to serve.

Hot Browns

Hot Browns are a very special sort of supper sandwich that originated at the Brown Hotel in Louisville, Kentucky. Including Kentucky in this book is a bit dicey, since the people who live there have definite Southern accents. However, Louisville is right across the Ohio River from Indiana. What's more important is that the food of Kentucky has strong heartland characteristics. At any rate, Hot Browns know no geographical boundaries. This version is a combination of ones from Kentucky (via my friend Ann Mitchell Hunter) and Ohio.

FOR THE WHITE SAUCE

½ cup (4 ounces) butter
½ cup flour
2 cups milk
½ cup grated Cheddar cheese
Salt and pepper

6 slices toasted white bread (or English muffins, split and toasted)
6 ¼-inch-thick slices cooked chicken or turkey
6 slices tomato (optional)
2 tablespoons brown sugar (optional)
12 slices bacon, cooked
6 tablespoons grated Parmesan cheese

To make the white sauce: Melt the butter, stir in the flour, then cook and stir for 3 to 4 minutes. Add the milk all at once and cook, stirring, until the sauce thickens and begins to bubble. Blend in the grated Cheddar, season with salt and pepper and set aside.

Now start the assembly: Put the toast or English muffins in 6 small individual baking dishes. (Lacking these, you can use a large baking sheet to hold all the sandwiches.) Top first with the chicken or turkey, then the cheese sauce. Now, if you wish to add an Ohio touch, put a slice of tomato on each sandwich and sprinkle it with a bit of brown sugar. Next, for either version, top with the bacon slices and sprinkle on the grated Parmesan.

All this can be done ahead of time and the sandwiches refrigerated. To serve, broil briefly until lightly browned.
• *SERVES 6.*

Chicago Deep-Dish Pizza

Pizza, in general, is hardly a Midwestern dish, but Chicago Deep-Dish Pizza certainly is. Back in 1943, a man named Ike Sewell invented this marvel and opened the first Pizzeria Uno restaurant, at the corner of Wabash and Ohio in the Windy City. Mr. Sewell loaded his pizza with a lot of extra cheese, plus chunky tomatoes and various combinations of Italian sausage, pepperoni, broccoli, mushrooms, onions, peppers, spinach, steak, anchovies, black olives, garlic, etc.

Today, there are Pizzeria Unos not only in the Midwest but also in such faraway places as Boston, San Francisco, Honolulu, England and Australia. The world loves Chicago pizza.

And the world would love to get Ike Sewell's recipe, especially the directions for his excellent crust, but it is as well guarded a secret as the recipe for Cincinnati Chili (page 30). I have heard that competitors have been caught combing through Pizzeria Uno's garbage, hoping to find out just what secret ingredients are used.

So I can't give you the exact recipe. This is my crust, not Pizzeria Uno's. I suspect theirs contains both durum wheat and semolina, not ingredients found in the usual kitchen. Mine's good, too, though. I've included quite a few of the typical Chicago pizza components, but you can add other cheeses or some of the ingredients listed above.

The biggest pizzas at Pizzeria Uno are nine inches. This one is fourteen inches, because that's the way deep-dish pizza pans are sold. Anyway, you might as well make a lot of this pizza while you're at it. Be aware, though, that, as opposed to the usual flat pizza, this is not a snack—it's a meal.

FOR THE DOUGH

1 package yeast
2 teaspoons sugar, divided
1 cup lukewarm water
2¾ cups unbleached flour
1 teaspoon salt
5 tablespoons olive oil, divided

FOR THE SAUCE

2 cups chopped onion
2 teaspoons minced or pressed garlic
1 green pepper, chopped
1 teaspoon oregano
1 teaspoon basil
28 ounces canned tomatoes, lightly drained (I use 2 14-ounce cans diced tomatoes), or 2 pounds diced fresh plum tomatoes

1 pound shredded mozzarella cheese, divided
1 pound Italian sausage, in bulk or removed from casings, broken up and cooked until light brown
3 ounces thinly sliced pepperoni
3 tablespoons cornmeal

To make the dough: Mix the yeast and 1 teaspoon of the sugar with the water and let sit until foamy. Combine the flour, salt and the rest of the sugar. Add 1 tablespoon olive oil to the yeast mixture and stir into the dry ingredients. Knead briefly until smooth. (Or use a food processor.) Put the dough on a lightly floured surface, cover with a bowl or cloth and allow to rest for about 20 minutes. (The short rising periods for this dough are not typographical errors.)

To make the sauce: Cook the onions, garlic and green pepper in 2 tablespoons of the olive oil until tender. Add the herbs and tomatoes and cook until the sauce is not at all runny.

For the assembly and baking: Oil a 14 × 2-inch round deep-dish pizza pan and sprinkle with the cornmeal. Roll the dough out to an 18-inch circle. Put it into the pan, pushing it up the sides, which should be a little thicker than the bottom. Brush with 1 tablespoon olive oil. Set aside to rise for another 20 to 30 minutes.

Now sprinkle half the cheese on the dough in the pan. Top with first the sauce, then the sausage, and pepperoni, then the rest of the cheese.

Bake at 425° F for about 30 minutes, or until the edges of the crust (which will have risen) are light brown. I was going to say that this pizza will serve 8 to 10. That was before 4 of us, including Meghan, my then nine-year-old granddaughter, devoured it with ease at one sitting.
• *MAKES 1 pizza.*

Vegetables

7 he Midwestern cooking of vegetables has been given a bad name through the years. You can see why when you look at such recipes as one from a late nineteenth-century Ohio cookbook which tells you to cook whole onions by boiling them in a potful of water for one hour, then draining them well, baking them, encased in buttered tissue paper, for another hour and finally peeling them and browning them in a little butter for 15 minutes.

There isn't much, if anything, which can be said to defend a recipe of that sort, but fortunately, hardly anyone cooks that way anymore. (However, see Indiana Green Beans on page 101.) Also, Midwestern recipes for most other vegetables have *always* been delicious. Dutch-Style Carrots in Cream, for instance, is an old recipe and a world-beater. as are the potato recipes for which the region is famous—and who could possible cook corn better than the natives of the "corn belt?"

Caramelized Fried Apples

You may be startled to see a recipe for apples leading off the chapter on vegetables, but fried apples are essential to Midwestern cooking, and they're used just as you would a vegetable side dish. You'll most often find them accompanying pork dishes, including ham, but they're apt to turn up with a meal of any sort. They are absolutely delicious.

4 large apples, preferably Golden
   Delicious, since they hold their
   shape and don't need peeling
3 tablespoons bacon fat (or oil or
   other fat, if you must)
⅓ cup water
⅓ cup sugar
A dash of salt (optional)

Quarter the apples and remove their cores, then slice them about ⅓ inch thick. (Alternately, and preferred by some, leave the apples whole; core them and slice into rings.)

Heat the bacon fat in a large frying pan and add the apples. Cover and cook over moderate heat until lightly browned, turning once. Add the water and sugar and, if you're using it, the salt and cook gently, uncovered, for 3 to 4 minutes more, until the syrup has almost disappeared.
• *SERVES 4 to 6.*

Indiana Green Beans

William Ruckelshaus, first administrator of the Environmental Protection Agency and former holder of various other governmental posts, is from Indiana, as is his wife, Jill.

I met Mrs. Ruckelshaus recently and asked her if she had any favorite and typically Midwestern recipes. She immediately started talking about the Midwestern green beans she and her husband both love. I hadn't had anything like them for years, but when I got home I cooked some according to her directions and felt a wave of nostalgia.

These beans bear little resemblance to the bright green, crisp al dente beans favored today in most of the rest of the country. Instead, they're soft and almost grayish, but imbued through and through with marvelous flavor. They're the epitome of down-home vegetable cookery.

1½ pounds green beans, trimmed, but left whole (or if pole beans, such as Kentucky Wonders, cut in 3-inch lengths)

1 ham hock or 4 or 5 slices of bacon (Mrs. Ruckelshaus prefers the ham hock because she likes the look of it "poking up through the beans")

1 medium onion, chopped, or 6 small onions, whole

Salt and pepper—maybe (see below)

Place the beans, ham hock or bacon and the onion in a medium-large saucepan and cover amply with water. Bring to a boil, turn the heat down to very low, cover partially—and cook ALL DAY! ("Like a Crockpot," Mrs. Ruckelshaus said, and indeed you could use a slow cooker for these beans.) Check occasionally to make sure there's enough water.

To serve, remove the ham hock. Now you can save it for another meal or skin it, chop the meat and return it to the beans. If you've used bacon, remove and chop it and return it to the pot. Taste to see if you need salt and pepper. You might well find the beans salty enough already, and pepper is definitely optional in this dish.

• *SERVES 4 to 6.*

Snibbled Beans

Sometimes it seems that the dominant flavor combination of Midwestern cooking is bacon, onions and vinegar. This has to come from the influence of the early German immigrants. One taste of their first dish made with bacon, onions and vinegar seems to have won over settlers from all the other countries and their descendants.

In Snibbled Beans, the bacon, onions and vinegar are mellowed with sugar and eggs. You'll find them succulent and marvelous.

6 slices bacon
1½ pounds green beans, Frenched (or use 2 boxes frozen), cooked and drained
1 cup very thinly sliced onion
1 egg
¼ cup cider vinegar
¼ cup sugar
Black pepper to taste

Cook the bacon in a frying pan until crisp. Drain on paper towels, then crumble. Put the cooked and drained beans in another frying pan, a large one, or a saucepan. Top with the onion slices and crumbled bacon. Set aside.

Pour off all but 2 tablespoons of the bacon fat; keep it hot. Beat the eggs, cider vinegar and sugar together and add to the hot bacon fat. Pour this combination over the green bean mixture and cook, stirring, over medium heat for 2 to 3 minutes, or until thick. Add the black pepper.
• *SERVES 4 to 6.*

Lima Beans Baked in Sour Cream and Molasses

These are dried limas, soaked, boiled, then added to a salubrious sauce and baked. Four generations of us in my family have made and loved these. They're usually served as a vegetable, but make a satisfying main dish, too. There's something about the combination of sour cream, molasses and mustard that suits the smooth limas to perfection.

1 cup dried baby lima beans
4 ounces (½ stick) butter, melted
1 cup sour cream
1 tablespoon unsulphured molasses
1½ teaspoons dry mustard

Soak and cook the dried lima beans following the package instructions. Combine with the rest of the ingredients and put into a buttered baking dish and bake at 350° F for 1½ hours, or until the top is bubbling and brown. • *SERVES 4 as a vegetable, 2 as a main dish.*

There's no salt in this recipe—nor is it needed. That's another wonderful thing about Midwestern cooks: Most of them only add salt where it's really essential for flavor.

Beets in Orange Sauce

Midwesterners like their beets to be sweet and sour—or at least sweet. Pickled Beets (page 196) are often found as a garnish or relish, and beets served as a hot vegetable are usually either bathed in vinegar and sugar or in a citrus sauce such as this one, which is guaranteed to perk up your jaded taste buds.

> 1 pound beets
> ½ cup orange juice
> 2 teaspoons finely grated orange
>   peel
> Juice of 1 lemon
> 2 whole cloves
> ¼ cup sugar
> 1 tablespoon cornstarch
> 2 tablespoons butter

Boil the beets until tender, then peel and slice them. Heat the orange juice and peel, the lemon juice and the whole cloves in a medium saucepan over medium heat. Now combine the sugar and cornstarch and add to the hot mixture along with the butter, cooking and stirring until thick and transparent. Remove the cloves, add the beets and reheat. • *SERVES 6.*

Illinois Broccoli Casserole

When I asked my Illinois-raised friend Nancy Duffy for Midwestern recipes, she came through with several great ones. Her broccoli and cheese casserole is a typical heartland treatment of this vegetable, too.

> 1 pound broccoli, coarsely
>   chopped
> 3 tablespoons butter
> 2 tablespoons flour
> 1¼ cups milk
> 3 tablespoons minced onion
> Salt to taste
> 2 cups shredded natural Swiss
>   cheese
> 2 eggs, beaten

Boil the broccoli in ample salted water for 8 minutes; drain. Now make a cream sauce by melting the butter in a fairly large saucepan, adding the flour and stirring over low heat for 3 to 4 minutes, then adding the milk. Continue to cook and stir until the sauce thickens and just comes to a boil. Add the onion and season to taste with salt. Add the broccoli and cheese right away, and stir gently until the cheese has melted slightly, then stir in the beaten eggs.

Put into a buttered 10 × 16-inch pan and bake at 325° F for 30 minutes, or until the center is firm to the touch. • *SERVES 8.*

Kansas-Secret Creamy Cabbage

In most households, Midwestern and otherwise, cabbage appears these days only as sauerkraut or coleslaw. The reason for this is obvious: Not many people want their houses to reek from the pungent aroma cabbage emits as it cooks. It permeates everything, and days of airing don't put a dent in it.

I learned the solution to this problem from a woman from Kansas. Just cook some green pepper with the cabbage and there will be almost no smell! Then you can make such fabulous cabbage dishes as this one.

1 medium head green cabbage, quartered and cored, then shredded
1 medium green pepper, cut in 1-inch squares
1 cup water
1 cup sour cream
1 egg, beaten
¼ teaspoon nutmeg
2 tablespoons sugar
Salt and pepper to taste

Boil the cabbage and the green pepper squares in the water for 5 minutes; drain. Now combine all the other ingredients in a medium-size saucepan, add the cabbage and green pepper and cook, stirring, for about 5 minutes, or until hot. • *SERVES 6.*

Danish Braised Red Cabbage with Apples

Similar dishes are made by the Germans, but this particular red cabbage dish is from the Danes in Minnesota. It's cooked by almost everyone now, though, and is considered the perfect accompaniment to goose or any wild game. I agree. I love it.

2 tablespoons butter
1 small head red cabbage, quartered and cored, then shredded
⅓ cup cider vinegar
⅓ cup water
1 teaspoon sugar
3 apples, peeled and finely diced
¼ cup currant jelly

Melt the butter in a large Dutch oven–type pan. Add the cabbage, vinegar, water, sugar and apples. Stir well, then cover and simmer for 1½ to 2 hours, or until tender (or bake at 325° F), checking occasionally to see if it needs more water. Now stir in the currant jelly and cook for 15 minutes more.
• *SERVES 6 to 8.*

Dutch-Style Carrots in Cream

These aren't, as you might expect, carrots boiled, drained, then doused with a cream sauce. Instead, they are actually cooked first in butter, then in cream, an old trick of Midwesterners of Dutch origin which makes a tremendous difference. All the glorious flavor of the carrots is there, enhanced by a gentle sauce.

1 pound carrots, peeled and thinly sliced
4 tablespoons butter
½ cup water
1 teaspoon sugar
Salt and pepper (just a little)
⅓ cup heavy cream

Combine all the ingredients except the cream in a saucepan. Bring to a boil, then cover and simmer until the carrots are tender. Uncover; boil off any excess liquid. Add the cream; simmer for a few minutes more, stirring, until the cream has thickened. • *SERVES 4 to 6.*

Braised Celery

Most of the celery used in the Midwest through the years has gone, along with numerous other vegetables, into soups or stuffings or appeared with olives and radishes on the relish tray, which seems to be an obligatory, though usually untouched, fixture on holiday dinner tables. The problem is that certain rather unpleasant dishes known as "stewed celery" or "creamed celery" have turned whole generations against the very thought of cooking celery. Now, though, beginning, I believe, in Michigan, the word is spreading that Braised Celery is wonderful. It was certainly a revelation to me. Its taste strongly resembles braised endive, a European dish I dearly love.

1 bunch celery
4 tablespoons butter
½ cup water (plus more to blanch the celery)
Juice of 1 lemon
Salt and pepper to taste

Trim the celery and cut the stalks into 3-inch pieces. Blanch in a large pot of boiling water for 5 minutes (this removes any overly aggressive celery taste). Drain. Put into a large frying pan along with the butter, ½ cup water, the lemon juice, salt and pepper. Simmer over very low heat, covered, for 1 hour, checking from time to time to see if more water is needed. • *SERVES 4 to 6.*

Omaha Corn Pudding

Another of the frequent uses of corn is in corn pudding, served as a vegetable. This version is from Omaha. (Iowa may be where "the tall corn grows," but Nebraska is the "cornhusker state." For that matter, you won't find a single area in the whole heartland where sweet corn isn't grown and served.)

You have to fine-tune this recipe a bit, depending on when you cook it. Early season corn, being juicy, may need the addition of a little flour. Late season corn, which is not as juicy or sweet, may need more milk and may be improved with a bit more sugar.

8 ears corn
3 eggs, well beaten
2 tablespoons butter, melted
1½ cups milk (plus an extra
    tablespoon or 2 for late season
    corn)
1 tablespoon flour (optional—for
    early season corn)
1 teaspoon sugar (or 2 teaspoons
    for late season corn)
Salt and pepper to taste

Cut the corn from the ears, scraping well to get all the milk out of the cobs. Combine all the other ingredients and stir in the corn kernels and their milk. Put into a buttered 2-quart casserole and bake at 325° F for 45 minutes, or until firm. • *SERVES 4 to 6.*

Or use a shortcut, as many do. My sister-in-law, Celeste Seton, has never, as far as I know, seen the Midwest except from the window of a high-flying place, but some of her cooking has distinct heartland overtones. For her corn pudding, just combine a 1-pound can of cream-style corn with 1 egg, put into a buttered baking dish and cook at 350° F for about 1 hour.
• *SERVES 4.*

Fried Corn

Most Midwestern sweet corn is served on the cob—and devoured with joy, several ears per person. Now and then, though, the desire for variety will enter the picture, or there will be a person who doesn't care for the mess involved in eating corn on the cob. For these times and people, there are a number of other great ways to cook corn. Fried corn is one of the favorites.

8 ears corn, uncooked
6 tablespoons butter
Salt and pepper to taste

Cut the corn from the ears, scraping well to get all the milk out of the cobs. Heat the kernels and their milk in the butter over low heat for 5 minutes, or until tender. Add quite a bit of pepper and a little salt.
• *SERVES 4 to 6.*

Eggplant and Tomato Casserole

While I haven't seen a recipe for this dish of my grandmother's anywhere else, it's quite typical of Midwestern ways to cook vegetables. Even my husband, who after twenty-some years of marriage informed me he didn't like eggplant, was fond of it cooked this way. (It's possible he thought the eggplant in this was apple.)

1 1-pound eggplant, peeled, cut in half lengthwise, then into ⅓-inch-thick slices
4 ripe tomatoes, peeled, cut into ⅓-inch-thick slices
Salt and pepper to taste
⅔ cup grated Cheddar cheese
½ cup soft bread crumbs
2 tablespoons butter
2 tablespoons water

Soak the eggplant slices in well-salted water for half an hour, then pat dry with paper towels. Place alternate layers of eggplant and tomatoes in a buttered baking dish, sprinkling each layer with a little salt, pepper and grated cheese. Top with the bread crumbs, what's left of the cheese and dots of the butter. Drizzle on the water. Bake at 325° F for 1 hour, then turn the heat up to 425° F for about 10 minutes to brown the top. • *SERVES 4 to 6.*

Crisp Fried Onion Rings

This is my family's version of how to make really crisp and sweet onion rings to serve with steaks or hamburgers. All Midwesterners seem to love onion rings, but, especially in restaurants, more often than not, the rings are deplorably soggy. Made this way, though, the coating is crunchily crisp and stays that way for quite a while. The rings can even be reheated hours later in a 350° F oven.

3 large sweet onions
1 cup milk

FOR THE BATTER

¾ cup flour
1 cup water

Oil for deep frying
Salt to taste

Slice the onions about ⅛ inch thick, separate into rings and soak in the milk for an hour or so. (This makes them extra sweet.) Drain, saving the milk to use in, say, a cream sauce. Dry the rings well with paper towels.

To make the batter: Put the flour in a shallow bowl and slowly beat in the water.

Heat the oil to 375° F and fry the rings, a handful at a time, until crisp, turning them once. Drain on paper towels. Sprinkle with salt. • *SERVES 4 to 6.*

Glazed Onions with Cream

Heartland holiday dinners aren't complete without an onion dish of some sort. You won't find a nicer one than this.

36 small white onions, peeled and
    boiled for 5 minutes (or use
    1½ pounds frozen whole tiny
    onions), well drained
4 tablespoons butter
2 teaspoons granulated sugar
A light dusting of ground cloves
¼ cup cold water
¾ cup heavy cream
Salt and pepper to taste

Place the onions in a large frying pan with the butter. Cook, stirring, over medium-low heat until the butter has melted, then add the sugar and continue to cook and stir until brown. Put the onions in a 2-quart baking dish and sprinkle very lightly with ground cloves.

Add the cold water to the glaze remaining in the pan and cook, stirring constantly, until a light brown syrup is formed. Add the cream and stir until it's somewhat reduced—just a few minutes. Season to taste, then combine with the onions. Bake at 350° F for 20 minutes. • *SERVES 6.*

Buttered Green Peas with Mint

Peas with mint often turn up as the simple green vegetable Midwesterners like to use to add spark and color to a meal. When fresh peas are in season, they're used, and there's nothing better, but at other times of the year frozen peas make an admirable substitute. The honey or sugar are added to bring out the flavor of the peas.

3 cups green peas, cooked and drained
3 tablespoons butter, divided
4 teaspoons chopped fresh mint
¼ cup water
1 teaspoon honey or sugar
Salt and pepper to taste

Just before it's time to serve, combine everything except 1 tablespoon of the butter in a saucepan. Heat, stirring often, and boil off the water. Then stir in the last tablespoon of butter. • *SERVES 4 to 6.*

In winter, when the mint patch is frozen, a tablespoon or 2 of mint jelly can be substituted for the fresh mint and the honey or sugar—or 1 teaspoon of dried mint can be used.

Scalloped Potatoes

There's not much difference between Midwestern Scalloped Potatoes and the very French gratin dauphinois—mainly just the fact that the French tend to add a touch each of garlic and nutmeg, while Midwesterners wouldn't dream of adding either one. They do use a little onion sometimes, though.

4 medium potatoes, peeled and thinly sliced
1 small onion, thinly sliced (optional)
2 tablespoons flour
Salt and pepper
2 tablespoons butter
Milk (see recipe for amount)

Layer the potatoes (and onions, if you're using them) in a buttered casserole, sprinkling some of the flour and salt and pepper on each layer. Dot the top with bits of the butter, then pour on milk until it's just visible through the top layer of potatoes. Bake at 350° F, uncovered, for an hour, or until the top has formed a thin brown crust.
• *SERVES 4.*

Cottage-fried Potatoes

Old Midwestern cookbooks and cooking notebooks don't contain recipes for cottage-fried potatoes (also known as country-fried). This is because they are so simple to make and were in such everyday use that recipes just weren't needed. They aren't in the new cookbooks either. (They aren't considered "fancy" enough.) Because of this, they've been a bit forgotten as the years have gone by. What a crime!

> 6 large boiling potatoes (or an
>   equivalent amount of smaller
>   ones)
> Enough bacon fat or other fat to
>   come up ⅛ inch in a large frying
>   pan
> Salt to taste

Boil the potatoes until just barely tender. Peel if you wish (I never do). Cut into ¼-inch slices while still hot and fry in the fat over medium-high heat, turning several times, until brown. Drain on paper towels and sprinkle with a little salt.
• *SERVES 4.*

Hash Brown Potatoes

Somehow, hash browns have stayed around in common usage better than cottage fries. Small-town restaurants and lunch counters are no doubt responsible for this, since the hash browns are just a shade easier to cook (mainly because they're usually made from cold boiled potatoes rather than freshly cooked ones).

Which is better? It's a toss-up. Today, I think I have a slight preference for cottage fries. Tomorrow, who knows?

> 6 tablespoons bacon fat or other
>   fat (or more—see below)
> 2 pounds cold boiled potatoes,
>   peeled or not, chopped
> Salt to taste

Heat the bacon fat in a large frying pan over medium-high heat and add the potatoes, pressing them down. Cook until a crust begins to form on the bottom (5 minutes or so), then turn them over as best you can and brown the other side, sprinkling lightly with salt. You may have to add a little more fat as the potatoes cook to keep them from sticking. • *SERVES 4 to 6.*

Swiss Roesti Potatoes

All over the heartland, people make browned potatoes to go with all sorts of meals, including breakfast. In New Glarus, Wisconsin ("little Switzerland"), though, they make roesti, known as the national potato dish of Switzerland. Doris Streiff, who gave me the recipe for Swiss cheese pie (page 92), also sent me the details of how they make roesti in New Glarus.

I was surprised. I'd been making roesti for years with just potatoes and fat (and loving it) and had been assured that this was the real Swiss way. Ms. Streiff's version includes cheese and onion. Hers is just as good as mine; it's just different.

So I'm going to give you the directions for both sorts of roesti. I recommend hers to go with any meal that doesn't already include cheese or onion, mine for any other use.

Doris Streiff's Roesti: Boil 6 potatoes the day before you plan to use them. The next day, heat 4 tablespoons of butter in a frying pan and cook 1 chopped onion in this until translucent. Add the potatoes, shredded, and fry for a few minutes, stirring several times. Now season to taste with salt and pepper and add ½ cup shredded Swiss cheese. Cook without stirring for 5 or 10 minutes until a crust forms. Now Ms. Streiff says to "turn with a spatula." I find this extremely difficult and suggest that you invert the cake of potatoes onto a plate and slide it back into the pan. Continue to cook until the second side is brown.
• *SERVES 6.*

My Roesti: Boil 6 potatoes for 10 minutes. Peel if you wish (I don't) and shred (I use a food processor's shredding disk). Heat 2 tablespoons butter, 2 tablespoons salad oil and a little bacon or goose fat in a frying pan. Add the potatoes, sprinkle with a little salt and pepper and press down well. Cook over medium-high heat until the bottom is brown, then invert onto a plate and slide back into the frying pan. Continue to cook until the other side is brown.
• *SERVES 6.*

Potato Pancakes

Potato pancakes were first cooked in the heartland by the Dutch and German settlers, then by the Jewish immigrants, who came later. However, everyone who tasted them demanded the recipe (or went home and figured it out), so they soon became a staple item in most kitchens. They're about as crisp as potato dishes come, and they're considered the perfect thing to serve with Sauerbraten with Gingersnap Gravy (page 26). Some people insist that they always be accompanied by apple sauce. But to me and lots of others they go well with anything at all.

6 medium potatoes, peeled and
  grated
2 eggs
2 tablespoons grated onion
  (optional)
2 tablespoons fine dry bread
  crumbs or flour
Salt and pepper to taste
Butter or bacon fat for cooking (see
  below for amount)

Put the grated potatoes in a colander to drain. Beat the eggs lightly in a fairly large bowl, then add first the onion (if you're using it), then the bread crumbs and salt and pepper. Now stir in the drained potatoes.

Heat 2 teaspoons of the butter or bacon fat over medium-high heat in a frying pan or griddle. When the pan is hot, put in 4 large spoonfuls of the potato mixture. Cook until brown on one side, then turn and brown the other side. Remove to paper towels to drain, then continue until all the mixture has been used, adding a little more butter or bacon fat for each batch. • *SERVES 4 to 6.*

Real Mashed Potatoes

You can't be a proper Midwesterner unless you know how to make real (as opposed to from-a-mix) mashed potatoes. Not only are they a necessity with any main dish that features gravy, but they're the beginning of many other creations as well—the following recipe, Mashed Potato Cakes, for example, Emergency Mashed Potato Soup (page 9) and even a chocolate cake (page 169).

"Continental" cooks say mashed potatoes have to be served the moment they're made. Midwesterners aren't that picky. They often make the potatoes ahead, put them in a baking dish and drizzle on a little butter, then reheat when needed.

1 medium-size baking potato per person
1 tablespoon butter (or more) per potato
1 tablespoon (or more) light cream or rich milk, heated, per potato
Salt and pepper to taste

Peel the potatoes, cut into quarters and put into a pot with enough lightly salted boiling water to cover them amply. Boil, uncovered, until very tender—20 minutes or so. Drain, then return to the pot and shake them over low heat briefly to dry them out.

Now mash the potatoes. The best way to start is by putting them through a ricer. Next best is to use a potato masher or a mixer. Don't try to use a blender or food processor, since they will turn the potatoes into a gluelike substance. Whatever method you use, beat in the butter and cream or milk and season with salt and pepper.

Mashed Potato Cakes

Here's the sequence of events leading up to mashed potato cakes: One day, you serve some well-sauced, wholesome dish which absolutely requires mashed potatoes. At that time, mash two extra cups of the potatoes and hide them in your refrigerator. Then the next day, or the day after, you're all set to make these lovely crisp-on-the-outside, soft-on-the-inside little cakes.

That's theoretically the way to do it. In practice, many a batch of potatoes has been mashed just to make the cakes.

2 cups cold mashed potatoes
1 egg, beaten
2 tablespoons finely minced onion
3/4 cup bread crumbs
1/4 cup light cream or milk
Salt and pepper to taste
Cornmeal or flour for coating
Bacon fat or butter for shallow-frying

Combine the mashed potatoes, egg, onion, bread crumbs, cream or milk and salt and pepper. Form into small cakes, coat with cornmeal or flour. Melt the bacon fat or butter in a large frying pan over medium heat. Add the cakes and brown on both sides. • *SERVES 4.*

Candied Sweet Potatoes

To many Midwesterners, if you have ham, you have to serve candied sweet potatoes, too. Much has been written deriding this exceedingly sweet dish, but it has its stalwart fans. It seems to me that if you're going to make the sweet potatoes, you might as well go all the way and have the melting marshmallows on top. These, again, have been an object of derision. I think guilt comes into this—anything this sweet can't possibly be good for you. True. But remember how much you've enjoyed marshmallows toasted on a stick over a campfire? It's the exact same irresistible taste. So go ahead, try this gooey and delectable dish and worry about your health and the state of your teeth some other day.

In some areas, these are called candied yams and the preference is for orange-fleshed sweet potatoes.

3 pounds sweet potatoes, boiled
   until tender
1 cup brown sugar
4 tablespoons butter
Marshmallows (optional)

Peel the sweet potatoes and cut them into ½-inch slices. Place these in a buttered baking dish, sprinkling each layer with brown sugar. Dot the top with little pieces of the butter.

Bake at 375° F for 25 minutes, until nicely candied. Last, if you're going to use the marshmallows, first level the top of the sweet potatoes as best you can with the back of a spoon, then put on a layer of marshmallows. Return to the oven until the marshmallows have melted a bit and begun to brown. (This won't take long, so check frequently.) • *SERVES 6 to 8.*

Spiced Mashed Sweet Potatoes

If you've made an unalterable decision against the Candied Sweet Potatoes above, then perhaps you'll try this different and delicious version of a sweet potato casserole to serve with your ham. The only sweetness here comes from the sweet potatoes themselves.

The combination of sweet potatoes, scallions, sour cream and spices is one of the few cooking touches I can trace with any certainty to the large numbers of black African-Americans living in the Midwest. In general, their excellent cooking seems identical to that of the descendants of the pioneers and the European immigrants.

6 fairly large sweet potatoes, boiled until tender, peeled and mashed
6 whole scallions, finely minced
½ cup sour cream
¼ cup milk
½ teaspoon nutmeg
½ teaspoon cinnamon
2 tablespoons chopped parsley
Salt and pepper to taste
3 tablespoons butter

Combine all the ingredients except the butter, then put the mixture into a buttered 3-quart baking dish. Dot the top with small bits of the butter. Bake at 375° F for 20 minutes, or until the top is lightly browned. • *SERVES 6.*

Spinach Puff

A puff is a soufflé made the easy way, with no separating of eggs and no careful folding in of stiffly beaten whites. A Midwestern concept, to be sure, and a highly successful one. This recipe, admired by all, comes from my son, Bob, and his wife, Kim, who live in Oklahoma. (Bit by bit, my family seems to be migrating back to the lands of its ancestral roots.)

¼ cup minced onion
4 tablespoons butter
4 tablespoons flour
1 cup milk
1 cup cooked chopped spinach (or use frozen, thawed and well drained)
A dash of nutmeg
Salt and pepper to taste
2 eggs, lightly beaten

Cook the onion gently in the butter for 5 minutes, or until just wilted. Stir in the flour and cook for 3 to 4 minutes, then add the milk all at once and cook and stir until thickened. Add the spinach, seasonings and eggs and put in a small greased casserole. Bake at 350° F, until puffed and beginning to brown on top. • *SERVES 4.*

Baked Des Moines or Acorn Squash

The winter squashes of the early days were primarily Hubbard, giant vegetables which had to be peeled and cut up before cooking. The Des Moines or acorn squash is a newer development on the winter vegetable scene, and one to which Midwesterners took an immediate liking. Its small size and convenient shape had a lot to do with this. All you have to do to make a remarkably good vegetable dish is to cut the little squashes in half, scoop out the seeds, put something interesting in the cavities and bake for a bit. The orange flesh becomes soft and absorbs whatever flavorings you put in the center.

Sometimes the little squash halves are filled with bread stuffings, or sausage meat or half strips of bacon are put into each cavity before baking. But most people prefer a sweet filling. This can be just a sprinkling of brown sugar or something as scrumptious as this:

2 acorn or Des Moines squash
2 tablespoons softened butter
½ cup orange marmalade
4 pinches of nutmeg

Split the squashes in half lengthwise and scoop out all the seeds and stringy material. Rub inside and out with the butter, then place in a baking pan along with enough water to come halfway up their sides. Put 2 tablespoons of the orange marmalade in each squash half, pushing it up around the walls of the cavity. Sprinkle with nutmeg. Bake at 375° F for about 35 to 40 minutes, or until tender. • *SERVES 4.*

Winter Squash with Dill

There's something about this combination of the flavors of winter squash, dill and sour cream that's exciting to food lovers. The recipe probably comes from the Scandinavian settlers, but everyone who's tasted it has proclaimed it delicious.

2 pounds winter squash (see below)
½ cup sour cream
2 teaspoons minced fresh dill (or 1 teaspoon dill weed)
2 teaspoons sugar
Salt and pepper to taste

You can use any winter squash, cooked until tender. In the case of acorn squash, use 2 of them, cooked in a pan with some water for about 40 minutes, as in the above recipe, but this time put into the pan upside down to preserve softness.

Using just the cooked flesh and discarding the peel, mash the squash well in a ricer, food mill or with a fork. (Don't use a processor or blender.) Combine in a medium saucepan with all the ingredients and heat gently. • *SERVES 4 to 6.*

Fried Green Tomatoes with Cream Gravy

It's not uncommon for Midwesterners to spend a good bit of time each summer and fall looking for green tomatoes that are just right for frying. A "just right" tomato is large and of a true green color, with perhaps a tinge of orange or pink. At that stage, it's more like a fruit (technically, of course, the tomato is a fruit), but has to be cooked before being eaten. Some green tomatoes end up in pies or relishes, but most of them are fried and served with cream gravy. They're terrific.

4 large green tomatoes, in ⅓-inch-thick slices
Flour for dredging
4 tablespoons butter or bacon fat or a combination
2 tablespoons flour for the gravy
1 cup milk—or a bit more
Salt and pepper to taste

Dip both sides of the tomato slices in flour. Fry in butter or fat over medium-low heat until both sides are brown. The outside of the slices should be crisp and the inside somewhat soft. Remove to a warm plate while you make the cream gravy.

Pour off all but 2 tablespoons of the fat in the pan. Add 2 tablespoons of flour to this and cook and stir until it's lightly browned. Add 1 cup of milk and cook and stir until the gravy comes to a boil and thickens. If you'd like it thinner, add a little more milk, but cream gravy is supposed to be on the thick side. Season to taste with salt and quite a bit of black pepper. • *SERVES 4.*

If you don't have access to any "just right" tomatoes, the usual half-ripe ones you'll find in supermarkets will do just fine.

Kansas City Stewed Tomatoes

This was the only tomato dish my father, who was from Kansas City, Missouri, really liked. It was, of course, the way his mother cooked them.

It didn't matter to Dad if you used fresh tomatoes or those from a can. All he cared about was that there be bread in there with the tomatoes and that the mixture be very sweet.

Use canned tomatoes if you wish—just plain tomatoes, not the canned ones called "stewed," which contain celery, onion, etc. If there's a lot of juice in the can, either drain it off or add enough extra bread to thicken. In the old days, home-canned tomatoes were served stewed all winter.

As you'll see, I've told you in the recipe to use bread crumbs or chunks. If you want the bread to be inconspicuous, use crumbs. But if you're making the stewed tomatoes for someone like my father, tear slices of bread into roughly 1-inch pieces. (In case I sound as though I'm making fun of my father's liking for this way of making this dish, I'd better add that this is the way I like it, too—because it's the way my mother, trying to make her husband happy, cooked it.)

8 medium-size ripe tomatoes, peeled and chopped (and seeded, if you wish), or 1 pound canned tomatoes, chopped but not drained (but see above)
½ cup (or more) soft bread crumbs or chunks
2 tablespoons brown sugar

Put everything in a saucepan and cook over medium heat, stirring occasionally, for 20 minutes, or until as thick as you want it to be.
• *SERVES 4.*

Tomato Pudding

Tomato pudding is another, slightly more formal version of stewed tomatoes, a bit sweeter, and this time cooked in the oven. I have heard that this was a favorite dish of that fine Midwesterner, Mamie Eisenhower (Mrs. Dwight D.).

1 1-pound can crushed tomatoes
6 tablespoons brown sugar, divided
1 cup cubed fresh white bread
¼ cup melted butter

Cook the tomatoes with 4 tablespoons of the brown sugar for 3 or 4 minutes, stirring until the sugar has dissolved. Put the bread cubes into a small buttered baking dish, pour on first the melted butter, then the tomato mixture. Sprinkle on the remaining 2 tablespoons of brown sugar. Bake, uncovered, at 375° F for 15 to 20 minutes.
• *SERVES 4.*

Quick and Tasty Zucchini

I'm breaking one of my own rules here. I've told everyone whom I've asked for recipes that I didn't want any that contained canned soup. This simple statement has, unfortunately, eliminated hundreds of recipes, among them some, like this one from my Illinois friend Nancy Duffy, that are extremely popular. Nancy suggested that rather than omitting the recipe, I substitute by giving instructions for sautéing mushrooms, then making a thick white sauce and seasoning it highly with onion powder, celery salt, and the like. At that point, I decided to relent and include just this one canned soup–containing recipe. (It strikes me funny that I was seriously considering substituting fresh ingredients for the canned soup originally designed as a substitute itself!)

4 cups sliced zucchini (or yellow summer squash)
1 medium onion, chopped
1 cup grated Cheddar cheese
1 can cream of mushroom soup
Salt and pepper to taste
1 cup crumbled saltines

Cook the zucchini in salted water to cover for 8 minutes; drain. Now assemble the dish in a buttered casserole by putting in layers of squash, onion and cheese alternately with spoonfuls of the undiluted soup. Season with salt and pepper. Top with the crumbled saltines. Bake at 375° F for 35 to 40 minutes. • *SERVES 4.*

Salads

and

Salad Dressings

Midwesterners eat a lot of salad, though they don't make a fetish of it the way, say, Californians do. It's just an accepted idea that salad is definitely part of most lunches, dinners or suppers. It's served at the same time as the main dish, usually on a separate plate, or afterward. If nothing else, there'll be at least some sliced tomatoes or a little lettuce with a simple dressing. Sometimes, especially in the summer, a chicken or meat salad can be the main part of a meal.

Many Midwestern salads are quite sweet. (My grandfather's favorite salad was simply leaf lettuce sprinkled with sugar. Try it!) Some are frozen. Some are both sweet *and* frozen, rather like the French idea of a sherbet to refresh the palate between courses. I'll give you examples of all these, plus some of the best Midwestern specialties such as Wilted Lettuce, German Potato Salad, Polish Vegetable Salad and a few of the favorite salad dressings.

German Potato Salad

German Potato Salad, one of the great Midwestern specialties, is served hot but somehow still seems a salad. We had it at least once a week, usually accompanying some plainly cooked meat—pan-fried sliced ham, for instance.

4 medium potatoes
8 slices bacon, diced
1 medium onion, minced
¼ cup cider vinegar
Salt and pepper to taste

Boil and peel the potatoes, then slice about ¼ inch thick. Cook the bacon until brown. Add the onion and cook for just a minute or two. Add the cider vinegar, then combine with the potatoes. Add the salt and pepper, then reheat over low heat, stirring gently. • *SERVES 4.*

Fourth of July Potato Salad

To me, the two things most evocative of Midwestern Fourth of July evening picnics are fireflies (often the first of the season appear on that day) and a potato salad of this type.

Everyone has his or her own little touches to add to potato salad. In my family, we always add a little minced sweet pickle and feel it makes a big difference. Others add everything from carrots to cucumbers to olives to garlic.

½ cup mayonnaise
¼ cup finely minced onion
2 stalks celery, thinly sliced
⅓ cup finely minced sweet pickles
2 tablespoons cider vinegar
1 teaspoon salt
6 medium-size potatoes, boiled, peeled and diced
4 hard-boiled eggs, peeled and chopped

Combine the first 6 ingredients in a large bowl, then gently stir in the potatoes and eggs. Refrigerate for at least 2 hours.
• *SERVES 6 to 8.*

Old-Time Macaroni Salad

People in other parts of the country think that pasta salads are a recent invention, but Midwesterners have been making—and loving—macaroni salad for as long as packaged macaroni has been available.

1 8-ounce package elbow
   macaroni
½ cup mayonnaise
½ cup sour cream
¼ cup finely minced onion
1 cup diced green pepper
½ cup diced red pepper or
   pimiento
Salt and pepper to taste.

Cook the macaroni until barely tender, then rinse and drain it and let it cool. Now mix all the other ingredients in a large bowl and carefully stir in the macaroni. Chill well.
• *SERVES 8 to 10.*

Kidney Bean Salad with Pickles

Midwesterners are often mavericks. They don't care what the rest of the world thinks on many subjects. They do what they think best. This trait turns up in their cooking, too—for instance, in this excellent sweet-and-sour salad. It's not so much the pickles in it that are startling to many people, it's the butter. Butter in a salad? Why not? There isn't much of it, and it adds a nice richness. You'll be surprised.

1 1-pound can kidney beans (or
   cook the beans from scratch)
1 small onion, minced
6 sweet pickles, minced
2 tablespoons butter
3 tablespoons sugar
6 tablespoons cider vinegar

Drain the kidney beans, but don't rinse them. Combine with the minced onion and pickles. Now mix the rest of the ingredients in a small pan and bring them just to a boil. Add to the bean mixture and chill.
• *SERVES 4.*

Camilla's Missouri Coleslaw

When I raved about her coleslaw the first time I tasted it, my Aunt Camilla, who's from Missouri, seemed startled. Evidently to her it was just a routine salad. Wrong, Camilla! I've never tasted a better coleslaw. Her real secret, which she relayed to me in the most matter-of-fact fashion, is the touch of juice from pickled peaches or watermelon pickles.

- 1 small head of cabbage, shredded
- 1 cup Boiled Dressing (page 133) or a bit more—you want enough to make a moist salad
- 4 tablespoons minced onion
- 1 small apple, peeled and chopped
- 2 teaspoons poppy seeds
- 2 tablespoons juice from Pickled Peaches (page 195) or Crisp Watermelon Pickles (pages 196 to 197)

Put the shredded cabbage in a bowl. Combine all the other ingredients, then mix well with the cabbage. Keep the slaw refrigerated until you're ready to serve it.
• *SERVES 6 to 8.*

Succotash Salad

Succotash goes way back in Midwestern eating, probably to the original denizens, the Native Americans. I've seen a recipe from one of the Oklahoma tribes which includes boiled winter squash, but the usual formula is just corn and lima beans. Succotash Salad is a more recent invention, no doubt occasioned by some leftover vegetables, and it's delightful. Like so many other heartland salads, it is prepared ahead of time, thus making life easier for the cook. (Midwestern cooks have always tended to be efficiency experts.)

- 1½ cups cooked corn, cut from the cob or frozen
- 1½ cups lima beans, fresh or frozen, cooked
- 1 cup tart French dressing (for instance, the sweet-and-sour dressing on page 135, minus the sugar and celery seed)
- 1 small cucumber, peeled and cut into small dice
- 2 tablespoons minced onion
- ¼ cup mayonnaise
- Fresh mint for garnish (optional, in season)

Drain the cooked corn and lima beans and combine in a bowl with the French dressing. Chill, covered, for 3 to 4 hours, then drain well (saving the dressing for another use) and combine with the cucumber and onion. Serve topped with the mayonnaise and garnished with the mint, if it's summer and your mint patch is flourishing. (Otherwise, you might want to use parsley.)
• *SERVES 4 to 6.*

Midsummer Sliced Tomato and Onion Salad

In the height of the season, Midwestern tomatoes are so beautiful and full of flavor that it would be a crime to bury them under a mound of extraneous flavors. On the other hand, a little touch of this and a little touch of that do help bring out the tomatoes' own flavor.

1 sweet onion, very thinly sliced
4 ripe tomatoes, sliced about
  ⅓ inch thick
1 teaspoon sugar
½ teaspoon salt
1 tablespoon minced parsley
1 tablespoon salad oil
½ tablespoon white or wine
  vinegar

Line a platter with the onion slices. Top these with the slices of tomato, arranged so they don't overlap. Sprinkle on the sugar, salt and parsley. Now combine the salad oil and vinegar and drizzle it on.

Allow to sit at room temperature for at least 2 hours so the flavors will blend. (The room temperature part is important. When you're lucky enough to get fresh, deep red tomatoes, don't ever chill them.) • *SERVES 4.*

Wilted Cucumbers

People in the rest of the country don't seem to cherish Wilted Cucumbers the way Midwesterners do (probably because they've never had them). Certainly, crisp cucumber slices are great, but once you've tasted the wilted dish, preferably served at your grandmother's table, there's no going back. These are used more as a "little extra" side dish than a proper salad.

2 medium cucumbers, peeled and
  sliced as thinly as possible
1 cup cold water
2 teaspoons salt
½ cup Sweet-and-Sour Celery Seed
  Dressing (page 135) (or omit the
  celery seed, if you wish)

Let the really thinly sliced cucumbers sit in a combination of the water and salt for about half an hour. (This will remove whatever it is that makes cucumbers indigestible to some.) Drain; rinse with plain water; drain again. Combine the slices with the dressing and chill until you're ready to serve. • *SERVES 4.*

Icebox Do-Ahead Salad

Here's a Midwestern salad with many virtues. To begin with, it's a green salad you can make hours ahead. (You have to, in fact.) Then, too, it makes its own dressing. And best of all, it's great-tasting. Use this recipe as a pattern, adding vegetables and cheeses of your own choice.

2 cups lettuce, torn in small pieces
6 tablespoons mayonnaise
1 small onion, very thinly sliced
½ cup other raw vegetables, chopped (green pepper, celery, etc.)
2 cups cooked vegetables (peas, green beans, carrots, or the like)
1 cup or more grated or julienne-cut cheese (Cheddar, blue or Swiss)
3 teaspoons sugar
Salt and pepper
¼ pound bacon, cooked and crumbled

You're going to make the salad in layers. Put ⅓ of the lettuce in a bowl, top with 2 tablespoons of the mayonnaise, roughly ⅓ of the raw and cooked vegetables and cheese, 1 teaspoon of the sugar and a little salt and pepper. Repeat twice, using everything except the bacon. Chill for at least 2 hours, but preferably a full day. When it's time to serve, sprinkle on the bacon and toss thoroughly, until the self-made dressing is well distributed. • *SERVES 4 to 6.*

Wilted Lettuce

It was a big shock to learn recently that someone I know, someone I respect, and a Midwesterner at that, actually doesn't like Wilted Lettuce. Could such a thing be? All I can think is that the Wilted Lettuce she's encountered is the kind made without sugar, or perhaps a version with eggs in it or even cream. Whatever sort of Wilted Lettuce it was, I'm sure it wasn't this kind.

6 slices bacon
2 tablespoons cider vinegar
1 tablespoon sugar
¼ cup minced onion or scallion
Soft-leaf lettuce (see below for amount)

Cook the bacon until crisp. Drain on paper towels, then crumble. To the fat remaining in the pan, add the cider vinegar, sugar and minced onion or scallion. Cook together for about a minute until it just begins to boil, then pour immediately onto the torn-apart lettuce in a bowl. Toss.

How much lettuce? Use about 2 or 3 times the amount you would use for other salads, as it wilts when the hot dressing hits it. In my house, every last little bit has always disappeared, no matter how much I make.
• *SERVES 4 to 6.*

Sometimes, when I get to worrying about the amount of saturated fat I'm consuming, I pour off half the bacon fat and replace it with salad oil. The one thing I won't do is stop making wilted lettuce.

Danish Salad

While this salad no doubt originated with the people of Danish extraction who live in the Midwest, it comes to me from the most unimpeachable source possible—my mother's recipe file. It's refreshing and pretty and can be made ahead—attributes that make it very popular.

Obviously, the advent of the food processor makes this a quickly prepared salad, too. Chop the vegetables separately and use a pulsing on-off procedure so you won't end up with a bowl of soup.

1 cup finely chopped cucumber
1 cup finely chopped radishes
1 cup finely chopped celery
½ cup mayonnaise
Salt and pepper to taste

Combine the cucumber, radishes, celery and mayonnaise and season with the salt and pepper. Keep chilled until you're ready to serve it. • *SERVES 4 to 6.*

Polish Vegetable Salad

"Eat your vegetables" has never been a needed admonition in most heartland households, especially when a whole gardenful of them appears in such salads as this. Those of Polish extraction make salads of this sort, as do Russians—and everybody else, as well (though some chicken out at adding the apple and pickle or fresh dill).

2 medium boiling potatoes
2 medium carrots
1 small parsnip
1 small stalk celery, minced
1 cup cooked peas, cooled (or use frozen peas, thawed)
1 medium apple, diced
1 small dill pickle, minced, or 1 teaspoon fresh dill
½ cup mayonnaise
Lettuce for serving
2 hard-boiled eggs (optional)

Boil, peel, finely chop and cool the potatoes, carrots and parsnip. Combine carefully with the celery, peas, apple, pickle or dill and the mayonnaise. Serve on lettuce leaves, topped, if you wish, with slices of hard-boiled egg. • *SERVES 6 to 8.*

Frozen Blue Cheese Mousse

This frozen salad from Ohio is usually served on lettuce with a meal, but it makes a lively appetizer, too, especially when accompanied by small squares of hot, crisp toast.

2 ounces blue cheese from Iowa or
   Wisconsin
1 3-ounce package cream cheese
1 teaspoon lemon juice
½ cup mayonnaise
Black pepper to taste
A dash or two of Tabasco or
   Worcestershire sauce
½ cup heavy cream, whipped

Combine the blue cheese, cream cheese, lemon juice, mayonnaise and seasonings, then fold in the whipped cream. Put into a bowl or mold, cover and freeze for at least 3 to 4 hours. • *SERVES 4 to 6.*

Creamy Meat Salad

One of the best reappearances of the many roasted meats cooked in the heartland is in the form of meat salads, especially creamy ones of this sort.

You can use any cooked meat—roast beef, pork, veal or whatever you have— but pot roasts and boiled beef are preferable because of their moistness. (And try a sauerbraten, page 26, salad sometime!)

2 cups diced cooked meat (see
   above)
½ cup mayonnaise or Boiled
   Dressing (page 133)
¼ cup minced celery
2 tablespoons minced scallion

Combine all the ingredients. Serve chilled.
• *SERVES 4.*

That's a very basic meat salad. To it, some people add an amazing assortment of such things as minced green peppers and/or pimientos, chopped hard-boiled eggs, parsley or other herbs, capers or diced tomatoes. (My own favorite version consists of just meat, dressing and about a teaspoon of celery seed.)

Ham Mousse

On the hot days of summer, few want a warm main dish, yet yesterday's baked him is sitting in the refrigerator, begging to be used. The most usual solution for this problem is to serve cold sliced ham, accompanied by a salad or two. Or you could use diced ham in a creamy meat salad, as in the previous recipe. But the most elegant reappearance of the ham is in a mousse. One of the main points of elaborate cooking in the Midwest has always been to show people you care enough about them to go to a great deal of trouble in cooking their food, and before the invention of the food processor, Ham Mousse filled this function very well. Today, it's hardly any work at all.

1 tablespoon gelatine
¾ cup water or chicken broth
    (page 51)
2 cups finely ground cooked ham
¼ cup finely minced celery
1 tablespoon finely minced onion
1 teaspoon prepared mustard
½ cup heavy cream, whipped stiff
Lettuce leaves for serving

Sprinkle the gelatine on top of the water or broth in a small saucepan. Stir over very low heat until dissolved, then combine with the ham, celery and mustard. Fold in the whipped cream, put the mixture into a wet mold and chill for several hours, until firm. Turn out onto a bed of lettuce to serve. • SERVES 4 to 6.

Chicken Salad with Grapes and Almonds

Midwestern chicken salads tend to be fancier than their meat counterparts. They're served at summertime luncheons and other dressy occasions and are considered a treat (rather than a way to use up leftovers).

This recipe is based on one submitted to a church cookbook about half a century ago by an Iowa woman named Truth Lamont. (When I was a young bride, I had the brilliant—I thought—idea of adding seedless grapes to my chicken salad. What a blow to find out that Midwesterners had been doing the same thing for decades.)

4 cups diced moist boiled chicken
    or chicken breasts
2 cups seedless grapes
¼ cup minced celery
1 cup shredded toasted almonds
    (or pecans or walnuts, in large
    pieces)
½ cup mayonnaise
½ cup Boiled Dressing (page 133)
Salt and pepper to taste (and some
    adventurous modern cooks also
    add a bit of curry powder)

Combine all the ingredients and serve well chilled. • SERVES 8.

Molded Fresh Fruit Salad

Fruit gelatine with marshmallows is a favorite salad in the Midwest. Community and church cookbooks are jam-packed with recipes of that sort. In the newer books, the salads are usually Jell-O and canned fruit all the way. This recipe, though, is based on some from older cookbooks. I think even food snobs might like it—especially if you leave out the marshmallows. (It may be true that you have to grow up eating marshmallows in salad to be able to tolerate the idea.)

2 envelopes plain, unflavored gelatine

¼ cup sugar

¾ cup water

¼ cup lemon juice

3 cups white grape juice (available in bottles) or pineapple juice

About 2½ cups fresh fruit, in small pieces (peeled, sliced peaches or pears, for instance, combined with raspberries or blueberries—or any fresh fruit except pineapple, which inhibits gelling)

½ cup miniature marshmallows or larger ones cut up with scissors (optional—depending on who's coming to dinner)

Combine the gelatine and sugar with the water in a medium-size saucepan and stir over low heat until dissolved. Cool a bit, then add the fruit juices, stirring well. Place in your refrigerator and chill just until it reaches the consistency of unbeaten egg white.

Now, using a 6-cup mold, arrange alternate layers of, first, the gelatine mixture, then the fruit and the marshmallows, if you're using them. Make the top layer gelatine. Chill until firm, then unmold onto lettuce and serve with mayonnaise or the Boiled Dressing you'll find on page 133.

• *SERVES 6 to 8.*

Frozen Fruit Salad

Frozen fruit salads serve exactly the same purpose as the sherbet served partway through an elaborate French dinner—both refresh the palate. Not that anyone thinks about this in the Midwest. They just plain like these salads. You might, too. Here's an especially nice one to get you started.

2 3-ounce packages cream cheese
½ cup mayonnaise
2 tablespoons lemon juice
1 orange, seeds, peel and membrane removed, cut into small pieces and drained
½ cup pitted and halved cherries (or use seedless grapes)
½ cup pecans
1 cup heavy cream, whipped

Combine the cream cheese, mayonnaise and lemon juice. Add the fruit and nuts, then fold in the whipped cream. Put into a small, fairly shallow tin. (The old recipes of this type say to use ice cube trays, but they don't come with removable center sections these days.) Freeze for 3 to 4 hours, or until firm. • *SERVES 6.*

Molded Cheese and Tomato Salad

My grandmother didn't make molded salads very often, but when she did, they were ultra good ones such as this. It's a sort of tomato aspic with a bland cream cheese filling, perked up with little bits of celery and stuffed olives, and it goes well with any meal.

1 tablespoon plain unflavored gelatine
2 tablespoons water
2 cups tomato juice, heated
1 3-ounce package cream cheese
1 teaspoon lemon juice
2 tablespoons minced celery
2 tablespoons minced stuffed olives

Combine the gelatine and the water and let sit for 5 minutes, then stir into the hot tomato juice. Put half of this mixture into the mold or molds you plan to use and chill until firm.

Now combine all the other ingredients and place on top of the tomato layer. Add the rest of the tomato mixture and chill again until set. Unmold onto a plate lined with lettuce leaves and serve accompanied by mayonnaise or the Boiled Dressing on page 133, preferably the Boiled Dressing.
• *SERVES 4 to 6.*

Broccoli and Bacon Salad

Midwestern cooks are often ahead of the rest of the country in using foods in new ways. I know Easterners and Californians, in particular (these people pride themselves on their innovations), will have trouble believing this, but look at this salad as an example. Spinach salad seems to have started out in the Midwest, then spread to the rest of the food-loving public, and then came raw broccoli, undiscovered by most of America until it started appearing on salad bars. I've even read that lemon meringue pie was invented in St. Louis.

This recipe, which comes from my old friend, Illinois-born-and-raised Nancy Duffy, will no doubt be appearing in New York and Los Angeles soon, though they undoubtedly won't use the sweet-and-sour mayonnaise.

1 large bunch broccoli
½ cup raisins, soaked in orange juice for ½ hour
1 small red onion, minced
1 cup mayonnaise
2 tablespoons vinegar
2 tablespoons sugar
12 slices bacon, cooked crisp and crumbled

Cut the broccoli into florets, reserving the stems for another use. Combine with the raisins, well drained, and the onion in a bowl. Mix together the mayonnaise, vinegar and sugar and combine with the broccoli, raisins and onion. (Boiled Dressing—page 133—would give you pretty much the same effect.) Chill for several hours. When you're ready to serve, add the crumbled bacon and toss gently. • *SERVES 4 to 6.*

Lemon-Cream Dressing

This is one of the simplest and most elegant dressings in Midwestern cooking. It's at its best on buttery leaf lettuce such as black-seeded Simpson, bibb or salad bowl.

¼ cup heavy cream
2 teaspoons lemon juice
½ teaspoon sugar

Combine all the ingredients. Mix with enough soft-leaf lettuce to serve 4. Chill until needed (but not for more than an hour or 2).

A nice addition, for a change, is the grated peel of half a lemon. Also, you can use sour cream, thinned down with a little milk, instead of the heavy cream.

Boiled Dressing

This is THE Midwestern salad dressing, used on almost every sort of salad by almost every cook. You can't buy it in stores, although certain bottled coleslaw dressings come close. I had mentioned in an earlier book that I couldn't seem to make a boiled dressing that tasted like my grandmother's. A kindly reader named Carla Hamilton took pity on me and sent me her recipe, and from this I learned the secret: Boiled Dressing doesn't need (does better without, in fact) the flour and butter that are in most recipes. This is Carla's recipe, and it's perfect, but I've cut the amount of sugar down. (She calls for ⅞ cup; you might want to try it that way.)

6 tablespoons sugar
2 teaspoons dry mustard
1 teaspoon salt
6 tablespoons water
6 tablespoons cider vinegar
4 eggs, beaten

Combine the sugar, mustard and salt. Add the water, cider vinegar and eggs and cook in a double boiler, stirring, until the mixture thickens and coats a spoon. Boiled Dressing keeps, refrigerated, for months. When you want to use it, add a little to some sweet cream, whipped or not, or sour cream. The proportions are up to you. Some add 6 or 7 tablespoons of dressing to a cup of cream. I prefer more dressing than cream, and sometimes even use the dressing straight, undiluted.

Sauerkraut Salad

Traditions passed down from the pioneers still persist in the heartland, though they're often updated to use today's equipment and the foods available now.

In the old days, just about everybody had a crock of homemade sauerkraut on hand, so this salad was a winter standby. Today, the Midwestern cook is much more apt to have a can or plastic bag of store-bought sauerkraut available, but the salad tastes just about the same and is still a standby, but a year-round one.

1 pound sauerkraut
¼ cup minced onion (especially red onion)
⅔ cup sour cream
Lettuce for serving

Drain the sauerkraut very thoroughly, then combine it with the minced onion. Let sit at room temperature for 30 minutes. Stir in the sour cream and serve on a bed of lettuce. • *SERVES 4.*

Frozen Tomato Aspic

There was a time when a ladies' luncheon wasn't complete without frozen aspic. Then, I suppose, everyone got as tired of it as they did of chicken à la king in patty shells, so it fell out of favor. There's a current resurgence, and I'm glad. It's always had an interesting grainy texture, and now the flavor has been greatly improved by using vegetable juice instead of tomato.

1 tablespoon gelatine
2 cups vegetable juice (V-8, for instance)
1 tablespoon lemon juice
A few drops of hot pepper sauce

Combine the gelatine with ½ cup of the vegetable juice and the lemon juice and hot pepper sauce. Now heat the rest of the vegetable juice to just below the boiling point and stir in the gelatine mixture, combining it very thoroughly. Chill, then pour into 2 or 3 ice cube trays (ones with permanent dividers, not the old-time metal ones whose inner sections can be removed). Freeze. Serve the little cubes on lettuce.
• *SERVES 4 to 6.*

Sweet-and-Sour Celery Seed Dressing

I think I was a grown woman before I tasted a salad dressing that didn't contain sugar. Eventually, I went so far in the other direction that my children never—at least at home—tasted a dressing that did contain sugar.

The sugar-laden dressings of the heartland are pretty darn good, though. The better of the commercially bottled dressings are, for the most part, attempts to copy them. To this day, the usual Midwestern idea of a French dressing is not a classic vinaigrette but a concoction containing sugar and often tomato. The tomato is usually added either in the form of catsup or canned, concentrated tomato soup.

If you want to try that sort of thing, you can add 2 or 3 tablespoons of catsup to the dressing below—or buy any standard pinkish or orange bottled dressing. I think you'll like this sweet-and-sour one better, though. Use it on a tossed green salad or on raw spinach, tomatoes or cucumbers.

2 teaspoons celery seed
1 tablespoon sugar
½ teaspoon dry mustard
½ teaspoon salt
¼ cup cider vinegar
¾ cup salad oil

Combine the celery seed, sugar and dry mustard in a small bowl or screw-top jar. Add the cider vinegar and stir or shake well, then add the oil and again stir or shake.
• *MAKES about 1 cup.*

Breads

and

Such

*B*reads, because they appear at every meal, are important in Midwestern cooking. They're also a big part of the area's heritage, and many of the recipes arrived in the covered wagons or satchels of the early settlers.

Bread seems to mean a lot emotionally to people. Midwesterners may be willing much of the time to use supermarket bread for sandwiches and even breakfast toast, but the breads served with main meals and for such entertainments as morning "coffees" are usually from their own ovens. It's a matter of pride. Sometimes these are yeast breads, but often you'll find quick breads, popovers, biscuits and muffins.

Certain recipes—Czech *Kolacky* and Christiania Kringle, for instance—are hard to classify. They're somewhat breadlike, but can also serve as dessert. Because they seem just right at breakfast, they're included here with the breads.

Two tricks for yeast bread making: (1) Use "Rapid Rise" yeast, ignoring the special directions on the package. (Use it just like any other yeast.) (2) On cold days, speed up the dough's rising time by placing the bowl containing it in a pan of warm water.

Batter White Bread

It was a great day for Midwesterners when someone discovered how to make fine yeast breads without kneading. This recipe produces a loaf which seems exactly like the usual biceps-building white breads, if not better. It's good for those who don't care for kneading and for those who are just beginning to make bread. It's good, period.

1 package dry yeast
¼ cup lukewarm water
3 tablespoons butter, cut into
   3 pieces
1 tablespoon sugar
1 teaspoon salt
1 cup boiling water
3 cups white flour, plus a little more
   at the end

Stir the yeast into the lukewarm water; set aside. Put the butter, sugar and salt in a bowl or a 1-quart measuring cup. Add the boiling water and stir. When this is lukewarm, stir in the yeast mixture. Now add this liquid mixture slowly to the flour, beating by hand or in a mixer. When everything is combined and the mixture is smooth, cover the bowl and leave the dough to rise in a warm place until doubled in bulk—about an hour.

Stir the risen dough until it deflates, then spoon into a buttered 5-cup loaf pan. (The usual Pyrex pan is this size.) The dough will be very soft and spongy. Pat the top of the loaf with a floured hand to smooth it out. (That's the only time your hands touch this bread until it's cooked.) Let it rise again, lightly covered, just until the edges of the loaf reach the top of the pan—about 30 minutes. Bake at 375° F for 45 minutes.

(The bread will rise an inch or so more as it bakes.) Let sit for a few minutes before removing from the pan, then cool on a rack. • *MAKES 1 loaf.*

Magic All-Whole Wheat Bread

To carry the batter bread idea further, there's this Ohio all-whole wheat bread which truly deserves the word magic. *It's magically easy, quick, firm, moist and beautiful. When I eat some of it, toasted, for breakfast, I feel full of vitality all day.*

3¾ cups whole wheat flour
1 package dry yeast
1½ teaspoons salt
1¾ cups warm water
2 tablespoons salad oil
2 tablespoons unsulphured
   molasses
1 tablespoon honey

Combine the flour, yeast and salt in a bowl. Now, by hand or with a mixer, beat in the water, oil, molasses and honey. Spoon the somewhat wet dough into a well-buttered 5-cup loaf pan. Let rise in a warm place only until the edges of the loaf reach the top of the pan—this will be in about half an hour. Bake at 350° F for 45 minutes. Remove from the oven, then let the pan sit for 5 minutes on one side, then 5 minutes on the other side before removing the bread and cooling it on a rack. • *MAKES 1 loaf.*

Limpa (Swedish Rye Bread)

Limpa, *Swedish rye bread, turns up all over the Midwest. (So do the Swedes themselves.) The molasses in it and the aromatic touch of orange peel and spice make it a bread you won't soon forget.*

    2 packages dry yeast
    ¼ cup warm water
    ⅓ cup light or dark brown sugar
    ¼ cup unsulphured molasses
    4 tablespoons butter, cut in 4
        pieces
    1 tablespoon salt
    Grated peel of 1 large orange
    2 teaspoons fennel seed
    1 teaspoon aniseed (optional)
    1¾ cups boiling water
    3 cups rye flour
    3 cups white flour (or a little less)
    A little milk

Stir the yeast into the warm water; steal a pinch of the brown sugar you'll be using later and add it; set aside. Put the molasses, brown sugar, butter, salt, orange peel and spices into a big bowl. Add the boiling water and stir. When this is lukewarm, add the yeast mixture. Now stir in first the rye flour, then most of the white flour. Knead for about 10 minutes. Put into a buttered or oiled bowl, turning the dough so all sides will be greased.

Cover and let stand in a warm place until doubled (an hour or so). Punch down, cover and let rise again. (This step is optional but helps the texture.) Shape into 2 long oval loaves. Put onto a lightly greased baking sheet. Cover and let rise once more. (Don't place the loaves too close together, as they will spread.)

Slash the tops diagonally in several places, French bread–style. Bake at 375° F for 25 to 30 minutes, or until a loaf sounds hollow when you thump it. Brush the tops of the loaves with a little milk, then allow them to cool on a rack. • *MAKES 2 loaves.*

Light, Delicious Yeast Roll Dough

Any rolls you make from this dough should win you a blue ribbon at the nearest county fair. It's a very nice dough to work with, too—you won't even have to use flour on the board when you shape it into rolls. Furthermore, the recipe cuts in half very easily.

If you wish, cut the amount of sugar down to 1 tablespoon when you're making nonsweet rolls.

1 package dry yeast
¼ cup warm water
1 tablespoon to ¼ cup sugar
4 tablespoons soft butter
1 cup freshly scalded milk (hot)
1 teaspoon salt
4 to 5 cups flour, divided
2 eggs, lightly beaten

Proof the yeast in the water along with 1 tablespoon sugar. Dissolve the butter and the rest of the sugar, if you're using it, in the hot milk. Let cool to lukewarm. Beat these 2 mixtures and the salt into 3 cups of the flour, add the eggs, then knead in as much more flour as you need to make a shiny, elastic dough. (Or use a food processor.) Place in a greased bowl, turning the dough so it's coated on all sides. Cover the bowl and let the dough rise for 1 to 1½ hours, or until doubled in bulk.

Use to make any—or all—of the rolls below, or whenever you have an eye on the blue ribbon. In all cases, place on buttered tins or in buttered muffin tins, let rise, covered, for 15 minutes, then bake at 350° F for 12 to 15 minutes, or until light brown. (The dough will rise more in the oven).

Round Dinner Rolls: The easiest variation, and one that's always well received. Roll out one batch of the above dough ½ inch thick and cut into circles with a biscuit cutter.
• *MAKES about 20.*

Cloverleaf Rolls: Probably the simplest way to achieve a fairly fancy effect. Put 3 little balls of dough into each of about 20 muffin cups. • *MAKES about 20.*

Parker House Rolls: Start out as for Round Dinner Rolls, but make a crease in each with a floured knife handle and fold over.
• *MAKES about 20.*

Sticky Buns

Sticky Buns, also known as honey buns although they contain no honey, make terrific eating. The only thing that's hard about them is keeping yourself from eating too many of them.

You can make Sticky Buns with the biscuit dough on page 148, and they're very good indeed, but most people prefer this yeast dough version. You might want to double this recipe. If by chance some of the rolls can't be eaten at the moment, they freeze well.

½ batch Light, Delicious Yeast Roll
  Dough (page 141)
4 tablespoons soft butter, divided
1 cup light or dark brown sugar,
  divided
¾ to 1 cup broken pecans or
  walnuts and/or raisins
About 1 teaspoon cinnamon

Pat or roll the dough into roughly an 8 × 12-inch rectangle. Spread with half the butter, then sprinkle on half the sugar and all of the nuts and/or raisins and the cinnamon. Roll up rather tightly from the long side. Cut into 1-inch slices.

Spread the rest of the butter in a round 9-inch cake pan, pie pan or skillet and sprinkle on the rest of the brown sugar. Put the slices of roll onto this, cut side down. Let rise for 20 minutes, then bake at 350° F for 12 to 15 minutes, or until light brown. Invert onto a serving plate so the sticky glaze will end up on top.
• *MAKES 12 large rolls.*

Czech Kolacky

Wherever Czechs have settled in the Midwest, and that is in many areas from Cedar Rapids, Iowa, to Cleveland, Ohio, to Montgomery, Minnesota (not to mention Prague, Oklahoma), you'll find the delightful little pastries known as kolacky *(pronounced "koh-lah-chee" and sometimes spelled* kolache*). They're most often made of a yeast dough (though some people use a cream cheese pastry) and have a filling resembling that used in a strudel.*

12 ounces pitted prunes or dried
  apricots
2 tablespoons orange juice
¼ cup water
½ cup sugar
½ teaspoon cinnamon
1 recipe Light, Delicious Yeast Roll
  Dough (page 141)
3 tablespoons butter, melted

Boil the prunes or apricots, orange juice, water, sugar and cinnamon together until the liquid has been reduced to thick syrup. Purée in a food mill or processor.

Form the dough into 40 walnut-size balls. Put them onto buttered baking sheets and flatten a bit with your hand. Let rise for 20 minutes, then, using your thumbs, make a wide but shallow depression in each. Put a heaping teaspoon of the filling into each depression. Bake at 400° F for 12 to 15 minutes, or until light brown. (Watch to make sure they don't burn.) Brush with the melted butter to make them shiny.
• *MAKES 40.*

Strawberry Nut Loaf

My Aunt Camilla Sternberg gave me the recipe for these marvelous little breads. (Aside from all their other great traits, Midwesterners are generous with their recipes. I phoned her one Sunday, asking for recipes from her Missouri background, and her answer arrived in the Tuesday mail. I knew Camilla wouldn't let me down.)

  3 cups flour
  1 teaspoon baking soda
  1 teaspoon salt
  1 teaspoon cinnamon
  2 cups sugar
  2 cups sliced strawberries
  1 teaspoon real vanilla
  4 eggs, well beaten
  1¼ cups salad oil
  1¼ cups chopped nuts ("Your choice," says Camilla)

Sift the flour, soda, salt, cinnamon and sugar together into a bowl. Make a well in the center and into this put the rest of the ingredients. Stir very carefully—just enough to dampen the mixture. (Overmixing will make quick breads tough.)

Put into 3 small (8½ × 3½-inch) greased loaf pans. Bake at 350° F for 50 to 60 minutes, then cool for 10 minutes before removing from the pans.
• *MAKES 3 small loaves.*

Mrs. Grigg's Orange Bread

Some people (I, for one) have been somewhat embarrassed by being unable to stop eating the orange bread made by Mrs. Grigg, the mother of an old friend. I'm lucky; she not only gave me numerous slices of her bread as we sat by her fireplace one cold afternoon, she also gave me the recipe.

  3 cups flour
  4 teaspoons baking powder
  Grated rind from 1 large orange (about 2 tablespoons)
  ½ cup sugar
  1 egg, beaten
  ¼ cup orange juice
  1¼ cups milk
  2 tablespoons butter, melted

Mix the flour, baking powder, orange peel and sugar together in a bowl. Combine the egg, orange juice, milk and butter (I do this in a blender, not even bothering to beat the egg first), then add to the flour mixture, stirring only until the dry ingredients are moistened. Spoon into a well-buttered 5-cup loaf pan and bake at 350° F for about 30 minutes. Let sit for 10 minutes before removing from the pan and cooling on a rack. • *MAKES 1 loaf.*

Michigan Graham Bread

If you like graham crackers (or even if you don't), you're going to enjoy graham bread. Like most quick breads, it's moist and rather sweet, and makes excellent toast.

Graham flour, made from the entire kernel of wheat, is available at many health food stores. Don't worry if you can't find it, as today's whole wheat flour is almost identical.

1 cup milk
1 tablespoon vinegar or lemon juice
1 cup graham or whole wheat flour
1 cup white flour
1 teaspoon baking soda
¼ teaspoon salt
1 egg, slightly beaten
¼ cup unsulphured molasses

Mix the milk with the vinegar or lemon juice in a medium-size bowl and set aside in a warm place until it shows signs of clabbering (curdling).

Combine the flours, baking soda and salt in a larger bowl. When the milk looks ready (somewhat lumpy), add the egg and molasses to it, then stir this combination into the dry ingredients.

Spoon into a well-buttered 5-cup loaf pan and bake at 325° F for 1 hour.
• *MAKES 1 loaf.*

Debbie's Pumpkin Bread

Midwestern kitchens are traditionally large, and it's a good thing they are, since so much goes on there. There's much cooking, of course, but also many family meals and a lot of just plain sitting around and talking.

There has to be a lot of storage space, too, for huge soup pots, Dutch ovens, roasting pans, cookie sheets and saucepans, frying pans and iron skillets of various sizes—and bread pans, even the collection of coffee cans needed to make such breads as this.

Debbie Kaczenski, who used to live in Wisconsin, shared this recipe with me. It's moist and gently spiced, and I find it one of the finest of all homemade quick breads—well worth storing all those coffee cans for.

4 eggs, lightly beaten
3 cups sugar
1 teaspoon nutmeg
1 teaspoon cinnamon
1½ teaspoons salt
1 cup salad oil
1 cup canned pumpkin
⅔ cup water
2 teaspoons baking soda
3 cups flour

Blend together the eggs, sugar, spices, salt and oil. Stir in first the pumpkin and water, then the combination of the baking soda and flour. Beat well, then divide among 4 greased-and-floured 1-pound coffee cans.

Bake at 350° F for about an hour. Cool for 10 minutes before removing from the cans. • *MAKES 4 loaves.*

Sour Cream Corn Bread

I remember the night in my childhood when my mother and Ola, who worked for us for many years, decided it would be fun to jazz up a corn bread mix in Midwestern fashion and make it taste really good. Here's what they did:

To 1 box of prepared corn muffin or corn bread mix (in other words, follow the instructions on the box, then carry on), add 1 egg, ⅞ cup sour cream and 2 tablespoons melted bacon fat. Bake following the package instructions.

If you want, you can make this moist and superior corn bread that way, starting out with a mix. Otherwise, here's how to achieve more or less the same results:

1 ½ cups yellow or white cornmeal
½ cup flour
1 teaspoon sugar
1 teaspoon salt
1 tablespoon baking powder
1 cup milk
¾ cup sour cream
3 eggs, well beaten
2 tablespoons bacon fat, melted
2 tablespoons butter, melted

Combine all the dry ingredients in a large bowl. Now mix the rest of the ingredients together and stir them quickly into the dry mixture.

Put the batter into a well-buttered 8½ × 11-inch pan and bake at 400° F for 15 minutes or a little more, until the edges begin to pull away from the pan.
• *MAKES 20 rectangles of corn bread.*

To make corn muffins: Make the batter for Sour Cream Corn Bread, above, and place by spoonfuls into well-buttered muffin tins or muffin cups, filling each one about ¾ full. Bake at 425° F for 15 minutes or more, until brown. • *MAKES from 10 to 20 muffins, depending on the size of your muffin tins or cups.*

To make Blueberry Corn Muffins: Getting up in the morning is easier if you know these treats are waiting for you. Follow the instructions for Corn Muffins, above, but toss 1 cup blueberries with the dry ingredients before adding the liquid mixture.

Christiania Kringle

Barbara Hornsby, a friend with a Scandinavian-Midwestern background, gave me the recipe for this good-any-time-of-day treat. It's a piecrust sort of dough, topped with a cream puff pastry and lightly glazed and flavored with almond. You could serve it for dessert, but it's at its shining best for breakfast or with morning coffee or afternoon tea.

For the pastry base: Cut ½ cup butter into 1 cup flour. Add 1 tablespoon cold water. Pat out onto a baking sheet, making 2 long strips. each 3 inches wide and roughly 16 inches long. • *MAKES 32 kringles.*

For the cream puff topping: Heat ½ cup butter and 1 cup water together until boiling. As you take it off the stove, dump in 1 cup flour and stir until smooth. Add 3 eggs, one at a time, beating after each addition, then stir in ½ teaspoon almond extract. Spread over the pastry strips. Bake at 400° F for about 45 to 50 minutes.

For the almond glaze: Frost the strips while they're still warm with a mixture of 1 cup confectioners' sugar, 1 tablespoon butter, ½ teaspoon almond extract and enough milk to make it spreadable. Serve at room temperature cut into crosswise slices about 1-inch wide.

Snap Doodle

There are many versions of coffee cake all over the heartland. This one's the best. (The fact that it's my grandmother's recipe has nothing to do with that assertion.) Snap Doodle is lighter in texture than any other coffee cake I've encountered. Also, while most such concoctions are made with butter and sugar mixed with spices and used as a streusel topping, Snap Doodle contains marvelous little wells of flavor all through the cake.

5 tablespoons butter, divided
½ cup granulated sugar
1 cup milk
1 egg, beaten
1½ cups flour
2 tablespoons baking powder
4 tablespoons light or dark brown sugar
2 tablespoons chopped nuts, preferably pecans
½ teaspoon cinnamon
⅛ teaspoon nutmeg (optional)

Cream 2 tablespoons of the butter with the sugar. Add the milk, egg, flour and baking powder and spoon into a buttered 10 × 10-inch pan. Sprinkle on the brown sugar. (Don't worry if it contains a few lumps; they'll just help matters along.) Next, sprinkle on first the nuts, then the cinnamon and, if you're using it, the nutmeg. Dot with the remaining 3 tablespoons of butter.

Bake at 350° F for 20 to 25 minutes, or until brown and bubbling. Serve hot—but it can be made ahead or even frozen and then reheated.

St. Louis Gooey Butter Cake

I've just written that Snap Doodle is the best coffee cake in the heartland. I think that fact would only be disputed in one place—St. Louis, Missouri. The local people there are wild about their own specialty, Gooey Butter Cake.

To say that Gooey Butter Cake is unprepossessing-looking is to be kind. It consists of a dry, flat base covered with, well, goo. It's chewy and sticky—and quite delicious. There are many recipes for it. Some, especially those made by bakeries and in supermarkets, tend to be built on a yeast-dough base. Most home cooks, though, make it starting with a box of yellow cake mix and say it tastes just the same.

This recipe comes from Elsie Sedlock of St. Louis, via her son Joe.

- 4 eggs, divided
- 8 ounces butter, melted
- 1 box yellow cake mix (use a plain 2-layer cake mix)
- 1 pound confectioners' sugar, divided
- 8 ounces cream cheese
- 1½ tablespoons vanilla

Combine 2 of the eggs with the melted butter and the cake mix, straight from the box. Mix gently, then spread in a well-buttered 9 x 13-inch baking pan, making a raised lip around the edge to hold the goo.

Now remove and reserve 2 to 3 tablespoons of the confectioners' sugar and combine the rest with the cream cheese, vanilla and the remaining 2 eggs. Spread this over the base in the pan.

Bake at 350° F for 30 to 35 minutes, or until the edges are very light brown and the top is still gooey. Let it sit for a few minutes, then sprinkle with the reserved confectioners' sugar. • *MAKES 1 cake.*

Cream Biscuits

Baking powder biscuits turn up in Midwestern life not only at breakfast but also as hot breads to go with main dishes, salads or soups. They can also replace waffles under such foods as Creamed Chicken and Ham (page 83), and they're vital in dessert shortcakes. Frankly, a lot of these biscuits are made from store-bought mixes. A lot, too, are made from the usual cut-the-flour-into-the-butter sort of recipe you'll find in most standard cookbooks. The favorites of many, though, are cream biscuits. They're light and rich—and very easy to make.

2 cups flour
1 cup cream or milk (see below)
1 tablespoon baking powder
A pinch of salt
2 teaspoons sugar (optional)

Simply stir all the ingredients together. You can use rich milk or any grade of cream, but for extra good biscuits that can be reheated, heavy cream's the one. Roll or pat the dough out ½ inch thick on a floured surface. Cut with a floured 2-inch cutter. Place on a buttered baking sheet and bake at 400° F for 12 to 15 minutes.
• *MAKES about 12.*

There are those who go even further and melt 4 tablespoons of butter in a 9 x 9-inch baking pan. They dip the biscuits top and bottom in the melted butter and bake them right in that pan.

Popovers

It's a firm Midwestern conviction that one of the most convincing ways to show your guests (or your family) that you really care about them is to serve them popovers. Making popovers can be a frantic business, though, with much desperate beating first of eggs and then of batter and the preheating of pans. This version eliminates all that and produces high-rising, perfect popovers.

2 eggs
1 cup flour
1 cup milk

Mix everything together gently with a fork or spoon. Don't worry about small lumps. Bake now or keep the batter refrigerated until you want your popovers.

To bake, fill small, well-buttered custard cups about ⅔ full of batter. Put on a baking sheet in a cold oven, set the temperature control to 450° F and bake for half an hour. (Or put into a hot oven and bake for a slightly shorter time.) • *MAKES 6 to 8; if you want more (and you well might), the recipe doubles or triples easily.*

Lake Owen Puffed Pancake

Lake Owen is a lovely spot in the North of Wisconsin. I'm letting it have the credit for this gorgeous baked pancake because it's baked and served there. However, it's also found in other parts of the heartland and is closely related to the apple pancake below, which is of Midwestern-German extraction.

> 3 eggs
> ¾ cup flour
> ¾ cup milk
> A pinch of nutmeg
> 4 tablespoons butter
> 3 tablespoons confectioners' sugar
> Juice of ½ lemon

Combine the eggs, flour, milk and nutmeg by beating well in a blender, mixer or food processor or, if need be, by hand. Meanwhile, heat the butter in a 2- to 3-quart baking pan or large iron skillet. When it's good and hot, pour in the egg mixture and put the pan in a 425° F oven and bake for 15 to 20 minutes, or until the pancake is puffed and gorgeous. Now sprinkle the confectioners' sugar over it and drizzle on the lemon juice. Put back in the oven for a few minutes to glaze. • *SERVE at once to 3 or 4. (In my family, this only serves 2, though. We love it that much. I usually have to make another or a larger one if there are more than that number eagerly awaiting it).*

Baked Apple Pancake

The Germans who settled in the Midwest had a tremendous influence on the cooking of the area. For one thing, they brought with them—and spread to their neighbors—a great love of vinegar. For another, the things they brought with them included the recipes for such delights as this puffed pancake. Follow the recipe for Lake Owen Puffed Pancake, above, with this small difference:

Peel and slice 1 large apple and cook it in the butter before proceeding any further. As with the Lake Owen pancake, be sure the butter is really hot when you add the egg mixture.

Deachie's Pancakes

Many mornings, Deachie, my grand-mother, woke me up by coming up to my room and singing, to the tune of "Here we go round the mulberry bush,"

> *"Lazy Glennie, will you get up,*
> *Will you get up, will you get up?*
> *Lazy Glennie, will you get up*
> *Will you get up this morning?"*

As she had trained me to, I sang in response, "What'll you give me if I get up . . . this morning?" And her answer came back, "Pancakes for breakfast if you'll get up . . . this morning." I got up. Deachie's pancakes were well worth emerging from the deepest sleep for.

These are thin, almost crepelike pancakes. For slightly thicker ones, add a little less milk. For really thick ones, see the next recipe, Paul Bunyan's Flapjacks.

1 cup flour
1 teaspoon baking powder
1 ⅓ cups milk
2 eggs
3 tablespoons butter, melted (and more for the cooking)

Mix all the ingredients together. (I give them a quick zap in the blender.) Cook on a hot griddle that you've greased with a little butter. (You know the pan is hot enough when a few drops of water sprinkled on it hiss and dance around and evaporate.) Use about a tablespoon and a half of batter for each pancake.

To make blueberry pancakes, sprinkle a few berries on each pancake just before you turn it. • *SERVES 4.*

Sometimes Deachie used buttermilk or sour (or soured) milk. In that case, she substituted ½ teaspoon of baking soda for the baking powder. At other times, she made buckwheat pancakes. In *that* case, she used Aunt Jemima's Buckwheat Pancake Mix, using more milk than the instructions called for. (Buckwheat flour was not something you could buy at the corner grocery store in those days; in fact, it still isn't. But you can find it in most natural food stores).

Palmer House German Pancake

One of the most exciting weeks of my life was spent with my grandparents at a time when my grandfather was a delegate to a Democratic convention in Chicago. It was everything you imagine a convention to be: bright shafts of artificial light, heavy smoke in the air, music, colorful banners, cheering and booing and an amazing sense of everyone being in constant motion.

Aside from the convention itself, what I remember best from that trip is the big rolled "German" pancake at the Palmer House, the hotel where we stayed. I can't imagine why or how, because I was quite young at the time, but I seem to remember that I had breakfast alone every morning in the big dining room downstairs. And what a breakfast—a huge, rolled German pancake. (Sometimes two or three of them, in fact.) Lots of people put fruit and spices inside such a pancake and serve it as dessert. The Palmer House proved it was my kind of place by using only sugar and lemon to embellish its masterpiece and by putting it on the breakfast menu.

3 eggs
¾ cups flour
1 cup milk
A pinch of salt
Butter, lemon wedges and
   granulated sugar

Beat the eggs, flour, milk and salt together until very smooth. (You can do this in a blender in almost no time.) Let the batter rest for an hour or so if you have the time. Heat a 10-inch frying pan over fairly high heat. Put in about ½ tablespoon of butter and tip the pan to let it spread all over. Now, right away, add ⅓ cup of the batter. Tip this around, too, and quickly, so the entire pan is covered. Cook until the top of the pancake looks dry and the edges crisp, then turn over and cook the other side briefly. Turn out upside down on a plate; sprinkle with a little lemon juice and sugar; roll. Serve with more sugar and a lemon wedge or 2.

• *MAKES 6 large pancakes.*

The Palmer House pancake was bigger than this, but most households don't have frying pans bigger than ten inches, nor do most cooks feel comfortable turning a pancake larger than this one. But if you do have a bigger frying pan and a little courage . . .

Paul Bunyan's Flapjacks

Paul Bunyan, a mythical giant of a woodsman, seems to have traveled, along with his great blue ox, Babe, from Minnesota all along the northern rim of the heartland—or at least his legend did.

To give you some idea of Paul's size, he was supposed to have greased the huge—to put it mildly—pan for his pancakes by having some of his henchmen tie sides of bacon onto the bottoms of their feet and skate around the inside of the pan.

Naturally, I suppose, a man of these dimensions liked thick, hearty flapjacks. And so do a lot of other Midwesterners. (I, of course, prefer the ones I grew up with, Deachie's.) Firm, thick pancakes such as these are known as flapjacks or griddle cakes rather than pancakes—a fine distinction, but I thought you should know.

2 cups flour
1 tablespoon baking powder
1 teaspoon salt
2 tablespoons sugar
2 eggs, well beaten
2 cups milk
5 tablespoons butter, melted

Combine the dry ingredients in a bowl or pitcher. Now combine the eggs, milk and melted butter and stir quickly, but not too thoroughly, into the dry mixture. (Overbeating makes tough flapjacks.)

Drop from a spoon onto a piping hot griddle or frying pan and cook exactly as you would Deachie's Pancakes (see page 150).
• SERVE in stacks of 4 or more pancakes per person to any lumberjacks who happen to come by. SERVES 4.

Fried Mush

It's tempting to call this dish by a more glamorous name, in the hope that those unacquainted with it would give it a try. But Fried Mush has always been its name and always will be. It's a breakfast dish revered over the whole heartland, and a wonderful one. The outside is crisp and the inside tender and melting.

There are two kinds of Fried Mush— one made with cornmeal, one with Cream of Wheat. They're equally good. My grandmother always made the Cream of Wheat version, but the cornmeal one goes back further in the history of the area. For either type, you have to make the mush the night before (or earlier) and give it time to chill and become firm enough to slice.

Both mushes are usually fried in bacon fat, and they're served with maple syrup or honey or the Corncob Syrup on page 199).

Cream of Wheat Fried Mush: Make Cream of Wheat, following the package directions. Chill about a quart of it in a 5-cup loaf pan. In the morning, slice the mush about ½ inch thick, coat the slices with flour and fry slowly in bacon fat, butter or other fat until crisp on both sides.

Cornmeal Fried Mush: I strongly recommend that you use a microwave oven for this. Combine 3¼ cups water and 1 cup cornmeal in a 2-quart glass measuring cup. Microwave on High for 6 minutes. Stir well, then microwave on High for another 6 minutes.

Otherwise, bring the water to a boil in a fairly large saucepan, then turn the heat down so the liquid is just simmering. Sprinkle 1 cup of cornmeal in very slowly, in a thin stream, stirring constantly. Continue to cook and stir for 15 to 20 minutes, or until very stiff.

As with Cream of Wheat mush, chill thoroughly in a loaf pan, then slice ½ inch thick, coat with flour and fry slowly in bacon fat, butter or other fat until crisp on both sides. • *SERVES 4 to 6.*

Sausage Scrapple (page 80) is a heavily spiced and meat-laden version of fried cornmeal mush. I think of it as a Sunday night supper dish, but many like it for breakfast.

Uncle Tom's Crisp Waffles

In this day of frozen waffles, not too many people make them from scratch. And what a shame, as the homemade ones are incomparably better. This is the way my Uncle Tom, a transplated Iowan and a man who doesn't usually spend much time in the kitchen, turns out a special treat for breakfast or for Sunday night supper. They seem to me just like the ones Deachie, who was his mother and my grandmother, used to make, and they're exactly what my father liked under his Creamed Chicken and Ham (page 83).

1¾ cups flour (use cake flour if you
  have it)
2 teaspoons baking powder
¼ teaspoon salt
1 tablespoon sugar
3 eggs, lightly beaten
1¾ cups milk
6 tablespoons butter, melted

Mix the flour, baking powder, salt and sugar together. Now combine the eggs, milk and melted butter and stir this gently into the dry ingredients. Bake according to the instructions that came with your waffle iron. • *MAKES 6 or more large waffles.*

Pies and Cakes

W hen you look at the tremendous quantities of desserts they cook and eat, it's amazing that any Midwesterners are able to fit through a normal-size doorway. Strangely enough, the majority of people in the Midwest are quite thin. (I do not recommend the consumption of many helpings of these goodies as a way to lose weight, though. I've tried it, and it definitely does not work.)

Desserts are what really count. They're the show-off dishes, the make-everybody-happy food. Many Midwestern community and church cookbooks, instead of starting out conventionally with chapters on appetizers and soups and proceeding through the rest of the meal to dessert and beverages, plunge right in and start off with the sweets. First things first. Not only that, they break desserts down into a number of categories (pies, cakes, cookies, puddings and so on) and have a lengthy chapter for each.

I'm restraining myself. Here are only a few samples of the fabulous Midwestern desserts (and I've allowed myself only two chapters for them), but they're such *good* samples. I hope you'll try them all. You'll find pies, cakes and frostings in this chapter, and puddings, cookies, ice cream and miscellaneous desserts in the one immediately following.

Buttermilk Pie with Orange Crust

Many Midwesterners are crazy about buttermilk. They drink it right down as though it were the nectar of the gods. Others would have a hard time downing a small glass of it. All agree, though, that when used in cooking, buttermilk adds lightness and a certain tang, and generally does wonders. Best by far of all the buttermilk recipes is this very special pie of my mother's. When served chilled, it's a lot like cheesecake—the most delicious cheesecake you ever ate.

FOR THE ORANGE PASTRY DOUGH

6 tablespoons very cold butter
⅞ cup flour
¼ teaspoon grated orange peel
½ teaspoon salt
1 tablespoon sugar
3 tablespoons very cold orange juice

FOR THE FILLING

1 cup sugar
3 tablespoons flour
¼ teaspoon salt
3 eggs, separated, whites beaten stiff
2 cups buttermilk
4 tablespoons butter, melted

Preheat oven to 450° F.

To make the orange pastry dough: Combine, by cutting in or using a food processor, the butter and the flour. Add the grated orange peel, salt and sugar, then the orange juice to make a firm dough. Chill for 1 hour before rolling out and using to line a 9-inch pie pan.

To make the filling: Combine the sugar, flour and salt, then add first the egg yolks and buttermilk, then the butter. Fold in the stiffly beaten egg whites. Pour into a 9-inch pan lined with orange pastry. Place in the preheated oven. Turn the oven heat down to 350° F immediately and bake for 45 minutes. Let cool, then chill.

Old-fashioned Apple Pie

This apple pie is old-fashioned because it doesn't contain any fancy flavorings or such gimmicks as cheese instead of a top crust or the addition of raisins or nuts. This is the basic old apple pie everyone's mother used to make—the one known as "Mom's apple pie" to millions and the one for which the "as American as . . ." phrase was coined.

Pastry for a 2-crust pie (see page 162)
6 flavorful apples (preferably Golden Delicious)
¼ cup light or dark brown sugar
¼ cup white sugar
¼ teaspoon cinnamon
1 tablespoon cornstarch
2 tablespoons butter
1 tablespoon water

Line a 9-inch pie pan with half of the pastry. Peel and core the apples and cut into thin slices. Combine the sugars, cinnamon and cornstarch and gently mix with the apple slices. Place in the pie shell; dot with little pieces of the butter; sprinkle on the water.

Put on the top crust; crimp the edges of the 2 crusts together; slash the top crust in 2 or 3 places. Bake at 450° F for 10 minutes, then lower the heat to 350° F and bake for about 35 to 45 minutes more, or until the crust looks done.

Ohio Shaker Lemon Pie

Shakers made lemon pies in most of their communities throughout the East, but the Midwestern Shakers at North Union Shaker Village in Ohio created a pie that was spectacularly different because it contained slices of lemon. In fact, aside from the crust, all the pie contains is lemon slices, sugar and eggs. And what a nice pie it is—Shaker simplicity and fine eating at their best.

2 large lemons
2 cups sugar
4 eggs, well beaten
Pastry for a 2-crust pie (see page 162)

Cut the ends off the lemons and discard, then slice the lemons as thinly as you can. (The Shakers said, "As thin as paper.") Mix them in a bowl with the sugar and allow to sit for at least 2 hours. Stir occasionally.

Line a pie pan with pastry and fill with the lemon slice–sugar mixture. Pour on the beaten eggs. Put on the top crust; crimp the edges of the 2 crusts together; make steam vents in the top. Bake on a baking sheet at 450° F for 15 minutes, then turn the oven down to 400° F and bake for another 10 to 15 minutes, or until a table knife inserted into the pie comes out clean. Allow to cool thoroughly before cutting.

Green Tomato Pie

The green tomatoes I've raved about elsewhere also make a terrific pie. Midwesterners don't wait until the end of summer, when there's a desperate need to use up unripened tomatoes, to make this pie—they go out and snatch tomatoes off the vine before they've turned red. It's hard to describe how good Green Tomato Pie is. It's a bit like an apple pie, but has its own distinctive flavor. You'll just have to try it for yourself.

8 medium green tomatoes, peeled, chopped and drained
Juice of 1 lemon (or 2 tablespoons cider vinegar)
2 tablespoons butter
1 cup sugar
½ teaspoon cinnamon
2 tablespoons cornstarch
½ cup raisins (optional)
Pastry for a 2-crust pie (see page 162)

Cook the chopped tomatoes, lemon juice or vinegar and butter gently in a medium size saucepan until tender—about 10 minutes. Now combine the sugar, cinnamon and cornstarch, stir into the hot mixture and continue to cook, stirring, until clear. Add the raisins, if you're using them, and remove the mixture from the heat. When cool, put into a 9-inch pie pan lined with half the piecrust. Top with the other crust; seal; slash a few times. Bake at 425° F for 10 minutes, then reduce the heat to 350° F and bake for another 20 to 25 minutes, or until the crust is light brown.

Kansas Pieplant (Rhubarb) Pie

Rhubarb was baked into so many pies in the old days that it became known as pieplant. The old farmsteads always had a rhubarb patch. Many people, and I'm one of them, love the taste of rhubarb. Those who only tolerate it, but perhaps find themselves in possession of a flourishing rhubarb patch, sometimes modify the taste by adding a handful of raisins or ¼ teaspoon of cinnamon.

    1½ cups sugar
    4 tablespoons flour
    4 cups rhubarb, sliced into ½-inch
      pieces
    2 tablespoons butter
    Pastry for a 2-crust pie (see page
      162)

Mix the sugar with the flour, then combine with the sliced rhubarb. Put into a 9-inch pie pan lined with half the piecrust. Top with dots of the butter, then either cover with the top crust (making a number of slits in it) or make a lattice top.

Place on a baking sheet and bake for 10 minutes at 450° F, then 25 to 30 minutes at 350° F.

Strawberry-Rhubarb Pie

Since strawberries and rhubarb are available at the same time of the year, and since they're such a wonderful combination, they're often used together in jams and pies. You'll find a recipe for Strawberry-Rhubarb Jam on page 202.

Cut strawberries into pieces roughly the same size as the bits of rhubarb. Use in any proportion you wish—half rhubarb, half strawberries, for instance. Cook exactly as you would a plain rhubarb pie.

Osgood Pie

This pie started out in the South, I believe, but soon landed firmly in the Midwest and has stayed there ever since. I've seen a version of it in which the name has become "As Good Pie," but "Osgood" is the real name, and it's an excellent dessert, rather like a light mince pie, with a thin, self-made crust on top. Probably the reason it was latched onto so eagerly in the Midwest is that it's a better version of the vinegar pies so popular in the area in the nineteenth century.

4 eggs, separated
2 cups sugar
3 tablespoons cider vinegar
2 tablespoons butter, melted
1 cup raisins, soaked in water to cover for 10 minutes, then drained
½ cup chopped pecans (optional)
1 teaspoon cinnamon
½ teaspoon nutmeg
½ teaspoon ground cloves
1 9-inch deep-dish pie shell, unbaked (see page 162)

Beat the egg yolks and sugar together until well blended, then add the cider vinegar, melted butter, raisins, pecans (if you're using them) and spices. Beat the egg whites until stiff and fold into the mixture. Put into the pie shell and bake at 400° F for 10 minutes, then turn the oven down to 325° F and bake for another 40 minutes, or until a table knife inserted into the center comes out clean.

Transparent Pie

Transparent Pie is a specialty of Ohio and Kentucky. That is, the name "Transparent Pie" is. I've seen a large number of recipes for it, and they are all very different from each other. In some, there's a layer of jelly; in others, the jelly is mixed in; some contain no jelly at all. In a few, egg whites are beaten and folded into the main mixture; then again, sometimes the beaten whites are made into a meringue topping.

And even the name of the dessert changes from place to place, in that it's known in some areas as "Transparent Pudding." This is because until well into the nineteenth century, one-crust pies were known as puddings.

The version below is a composite, created by me from a consensus of the recipes I've seen. Since it's based primarily on the oldest recipes, you could call it a pudding, if that appeals to you. But by any name, you'll find this a fine dessert, with a brown top, a translucent (rather than transparent) middle and a layer of tart jelly on the bottom.

1 cup sugar
1 cup (2 sticks) butter
3 eggs
1 teaspoon vanilla
½ cup tart jelly (e.g., currant)
1 9-inch deep-dish pie shell, unbaked (see page 162)

Cream the sugar and butter until fluffy, then add the eggs and beat (and beat and beat) until very light. Add the vanilla. Spread the jelly in the bottom of the pie shell and top with the beaten mixture, spreading it out well. Bake at 450° F for 5 minutes, then turn the heat down to 350° F and bake for another 20 to 25 minutes, or until the top is brown and the filling has set. Allow to cool before cutting, to give the jelly a chance to resolidify.

Chocolate Chip Walnut Pie

When I asked my Aunt Camilla for some Midwestern recipes, I didn't expect anything like what she sent me. After all, she's as thin as the model she used to be and very diet-conscious. But she sent me an envelope full of recipes for gorgeous, gooey and extremely fattening foods. They're extremely good, too, and very Midwestern. Testing them hasn't helped my waistline a bit, but eating them has been quite a pleasure. This pie, in particular, is a dazzler.

2 eggs
½ cup granulated sugar
½ cup light or dark brown sugar,
   firmly packed
1 cup (2 sticks) butter, melted, then
   cooled to room temperature
1 6-ounce package chocolate
   chips
1 cup chopped walnuts
1 9-inch deep-dish pie shell,
   unbaked (see page 162)

Beat the eggs in a large bowl until foamy, then add both sugars and beat until very well blended. Beat in the melted butter, then fold in the chocolate chips and walnuts.

Spoon into the pie shell and bake at 325° F for 1 hour, or until a table knife inserted in the center comes out clean.

Because my daughter Candace doesn't like walnuts, I've also made this for her with pecans. The verdict: Wow.

Macaroon Pie

Saltines are the secret weapon of Midwestern cooking. They are used for breading, they turn up in scalloped dishes, they even substitute for fruit in the amazing dish called Mock Apple Pie (see the following recipe). In Macaroon Pie, saltines are magically transformed, with the help of a few other ingredients, into a very nice almond-flavored macaroonlike dessert.

        3 egg whites
        1 cup sugar
        1/3 cup cracker crumbs (about
            27 single saltines, crushed)
        1 teaspoon baking powder
        1/2 teaspoon almond extract
        Whipped cream (optional)
        Shaved bittersweet chocolate
            (optional)

Beat the egg whites just until foamy, then slowly beat in the sugar and keep on beating until the mixture stands in soft peaks. Combine the cracker crumbs and baking powder, then fold into the egg whites. Next, fold in the almond extract. Spread the meringuelike mixture out in a well-buttered and floured 9-inch pie pan. Bake at 300° F for 45 minutes, or until set and just beginning to take on color. Let it cool completely before removing from the pan. Serve at room temperature topped with, if you like, whipped cream and perhaps shaved bittersweet chocolate.

Mock Apple Pie

Mock Apple Pie is a very good fraud. Many a Midwesterner actually prefers this version to the real apple pie.

To make it: Follow the directions for the preceding recipe, Macaroon Pie, but add 1/2 cup chopped nuts and 1/2 teaspoon cinnamon and use vanilla instead of almond extract.

Perfect Piecrust

Perfect Piecrust is tender, flaky, and easy to handle. Here's how to do it. Use all butter or margarine, if you prefer, but a lard crust is flaky, ultra Midwestern and just right. To make enough for a 1-crust pie, use half of all the ingredients.

        6 tablespoons very cold butter
        6 tablespoons very cold lard
        1 3/4 cups flour
        1 teaspoon salt
        6 tablespoons ice-cold water

Combine, by cutting in or using a food processor, the butter, lard, flour and salt. Add the ice-cold water. Chill at least 1 hour before rolling out. • *MAKES enough for a 2-crust deep-dish pie.*

If you're afraid of having a soggy bottom crust you can, even if the recipe specifies an unbaked crust, partially prebake it before filling—or simply place the filled pie on a heavy cookie sheet to bake.

Mrs. J. W. Millette's Jam Cake

Nancy Millette Mosher, whose mother's recipe this is, says this was the cake she always asked for, and got, for her birthday when she was growing up in Dayton, Ohio. Her eyes still light up when she talks about it, and now that I've tried it, I can see why. Nancy was a lucky little girl.

½ cup butter
1 cup brown sugar
2 eggs
1 cup strawberry jam
1¾ cups flour
1 teaspoon baking soda
¼ cup sour milk (or ¼ cup sweet milk, warm, combined with 1 teaspoon lemon juice)

FOR THE CARAMEL ICING

2 cups light brown sugar
½ cup rich milk or heavy cream
2½ tablespoons butter

Cream the butter and brown sugar, then beat in first the eggs, then the jam. Combine the flour and baking soda and add to the batter in small amounts alternately with spoonfuls of the milk. (Since I can't stay in the same room with naturally soured milk, I always do the lemon juice trick.)

Bake in 2 well-buttered cake pans at 350° F for about 30 minutes. When cool, fill and frost with Nancy's mother's caramel icing, below, or use a simple buttercream such as the one on pages 170 to 171.

To make the caramel icing: Combine the light brown sugar, rich milk or cream and butter in a saucepan. Bring to a boil, stirring. Continue to cook to the soft-boil stage (238° F), then beat until cool.

I've seen other recipes for jam cakes, but they all involve heavy measures of various spices and vanilla and call for a dark jam such as blackberry. Mrs. Millette, who was a remarkable woman in other ways, too (she was writing about women's rights late in the nineteenth century), let the flavor of the jam stand by itself for a moist yet delicate cake with a definite taste of strawberries.

Fabulous Chocolate Cake

Back around 1940 or so, a cousin of my family's friend Roberta McCoid had a piece of chocolate cake at one of Chicago's better restaurants. She liked it so much that when she got back home (to Iowa, I believe), she wrote to the restaurant and asked for the recipe, adding, "Naturally, I expect to pay for this." By return mail, she received the recipe—and a bill for $100. Lawyers in her family told her she had no choice but to pay. (I imagine they also had a few words for her on the subject of "setting yourself up.") She sent off her $100, but avenged herself by spreading the recipe as far and wide as she could. Even at this late date, I'm happy to help. It truly is a fabulous cake.

4 ounces unsweetened chocolate
1 cup (2 sticks) butter
2 cups sugar
2 eggs, beaten
2 teaspoons baking powder
2 cups flour
1½ cups milk
2 teaspoons vanilla
1 cup chopped pecans or walnuts

FOR THE FABULOUS FROSTING

¼ pound butter
2 ounces unsweetened chocolate
1 egg, beaten
2½ cups confectioners' sugar
1 tablespoon vanilla
2 tablespoons lemon juice
1 cup chopped pecans or walnuts

Melt the chocolate and let it cool slightly while you cream the butter and sugar. Now add to this first the eggs, then the melted chocolate. Next, combine the baking powder and flour and add to the chocolate mixture in small amounts alternately with small amounts of the milk. Add the vanilla and nuts last.

Bake in a buttered 9 × 9-inch pan at 350° F for 25 to 30 minutes. (I've also seen this cake baked in layers, and I believe the original recipe says to use a loaf pan.)

To make the fabulous frosting: (This was part of the original recipe from the Chicago restaurant and is easily worth $100 all by itself.) Melt the butter with the unsweetened chocolate. Add the beaten egg, then alternately, in small amounts, the confectioners' sugar, vanilla, lemon juice (that's the real stroke of genius) and chopped nuts.

In the interests of economy or calorie sparing, or because you're out of them, you could eliminate the nuts from the cake and/or the frosting. No great harm would be done. (Well, you might have lowered a $100 recipe down to about $82.50, but that's all right.)

Chocolate Upside-down Cake

Chocolate Upside-down Cake is one of the Midwestern desserts that my mother— thank goodness—kept on cooking when we moved East. It's an amazing recipe, more of a pudding than a cake, and you have to wonder how it ever came to be invented. You pour a thin liquid mixture over the cake batter before baking, and somehow it works its way through to the bottom, thickens and becomes a lovely rich sauce. Mother used to serve it for elaborate dinner parties as well as family meals.

Commercial mix makers have tried to approximate a pudding cake of this sort. Their method is the same, but the result doesn't come close.

1 cup flour
2 teaspoons baking powder
¾ cup sugar
2 tablespoons butter
1 ounce unsweetened chocolate
½ cup milk
½ cup coarsely chopped pecans (optional)
1 teaspoon pure vanilla
Whipped cream (optional)

FOR THE SAUCE

½ cup white sugar
½ cup light brown sugar
3 tablespoons cocoa
1 cup cold water

Combine the flour, baking powder and sugar in a large bowl. Melt the butter and chocolate together. Beat the milk into the flour mixture, then beat in the chocolate combination, the nuts, if you're using them, and the vanilla. Put into a buttered 8 × 8-inch pan.

To make the sauce: Combine the sugars and cocoa. Slowly stir in the cold water, then carefully spoon the mixture over the cake batter in the pan.

Bake for 40 minutes at 375° F. Put the pan on a rack until thoroughly cool, then invert it into a serving dish. A little whipped cream served with this is a nice touch.

Scripture Cake

Get out your old family Bible. (Or don't, if you don't feel like puzzle solving while cooking—I'll give you a translation below.) Scripture Cake, which is in dozens of community cookbooks from throughout the heartland, goes back to the early nineteenth century and is an example of the Midwestern sense of humor. (Somewhat to my surprise, it turns out to be a very nice fruit-filled cake, too.) Here's how it usually appears in the books:

1 cup Judges 5:25
3½ cups I Kings 4:22
2 teaspoons Amos 4:5
3 cups Jeremiah 6:20
2 cups I Samuel 30:12
2 cups I Jeremiah 24:2
1 cup Numbers 10:14
6 Isaiah 10:14
1 tablespoon Genesis 43:11
1 pinch Leviticus 2:13
I Kings 10:10

Mix as usual.

That makes fun reading, I think. For those who'd like to try the cake without spending hours of Bible study to learn such things as that butter is mentioned in Judges 5:24, here's the translation:

1 cup butter
3½ cups flour
2 teaspoons baking powder
3 cups sugar
2 cups raisins
2 cups chopped figs (substitute dates or dried apricots, if you wish)
1 cup water (but milk is sometimes substituted)
6 eggs
1 tablespoon honey
1 pinch salt
Spices to taste (try 2 teaspoons mixed spices or pumpkin pie spice)

Now for "mix as usual," which in a way is the most delightful part of the whole crazy recipe. The ingredients are not listed in the usual order-of-use manner. You'll have to skip around a bit.

Cream the butter with the sugar until light and fluffy. Beat the eggs into this, one at a time, then the honey. Take about ½ cup of the flour and mix it with the dried fruits. Set aside. Combine the rest of the flour with the baking powder, sugar, salt and spices and beat into the egg mixture alternately with the milk or water. Fold in the flour-coated fruits.

You have now "mixed as usual." You'll notice that the recipe doesn't mention anything about baking, let alone shaping, but what we're after is loaf cakes. Divide the batter between 2 large or 4 small well-buttered loaf pans. Bake at 300° F for 1½ to 2 hours, or until the cakes shrink from the edges of the pans.

Put the pans on a rack, on their sides. After 20 minutes, shift them so they rest on the other side. Don't remove the cakes from the pans until cool.

Mint-Chocolate Shadow Cake

This is without doubt my very favorite cake. I wish someone would make it for me for my birthday. (My chances aren't bad, since I'm sure both my daughters, Katie and Candace, will read this book—and they're both good cooks, like their Mid-western forebears.) The bitter chocolate on top of the mint frosting is what creates the shadow and what makes it so delectable.

You don't need any special recipe for shadow cake, just general instructions:

Make any chocolate cake. It can be a layer cake or one made in a tube pan. When it's cool, put it on a plate or a cake stand.

Frost with Fluffy White Frosting (page 171) to which you've added a few drops of mint extract to taste.

Now melt 2 ounces of unsweetened baking chocolate and pour on top of the white frosting. The idea is for the chocolate to cover the top of the cake and drip down the sides. Keep refrigerated so the thin layer of chocolate will remain crisp.

Mystery Cake

The heartland is always full of surprises. One day, I was driving through the Missouri countryside and glanced up at a hillside—to find it was dotted here and there with camels! *(They were parked there during the off-season of a circus.) And now I read that there are more than 100 Midwestern farmers who are raising* ostriches!

So it should come as no shock to find a cake that contains tomato soup. It's a good cake, too, moist and tasty, but I suspect its originator was wise to call it "Mystery Cake" rather than "Tomato Soup Cake."

4 tablespoons butter
1 cup sugar
2 eggs
2 cups flour
1 cup raisins
1 cup chopped pecans or walnuts
1 teaspoon baking soda
½ teaspoon salt
1 teaspoon cinnamon
1 teaspoon nutmeg
⅛ teaspoon ground cloves
1 10¾-ounce can tomato soup, undiluted
½ cup confectioners' sugar

Cream the butter and sugar together until light and fluffy, then beat in the eggs, one at a time. Toss about ¼ cup of the flour with the raisins and nuts and set aside. Now combine the rest of the flour with the baking soda, salt and spices and add this alternately with the tomato soup to the butter-sugar-egg mixture. Stir in the raisins and nuts.

Spoon into a well-buttered 9-inch tube (angel food cake) pan and bake at 350° F for 45 minutes, or until the top springs back when you touch it lightly. When cool, sprinkle with confectioners' sugar.

Chocolate Mashed Potato Cake

Mashed potatoes in a cake? Why not? They add a great deal of moistness (and besides, it's a way to use up leftover mashed potatoes). This cake has never, as far as I know, been given another name, one that would conceal its surprise ingredient. (People are probably more ready to accept the idea of potatoes in their cake than tomato soup, the mystery ingredient of the previous recipe.) This is a Kansas recipe, representative of others from throughout the heartland.

½ cup milk
2 ounces unsweetened baking
  chocolate
1 cup (2 sticks) butter
2 cups sugar
1 cup mashed potatoes, freshly
  made or leftover
4 eggs, separated
2 cups cake flour
2 teaspoons baking powder
½ teaspoon cinnamon
¼ teaspoon ground cloves
1 teaspoon pure vanilla

Cook the milk and chocolate gently together in a small saucepan until the chocolate has melted. Put aside for now. Cream the butter and sugar together, then beat in the mashed potatoes. Beat the egg yolks slightly and stir them in. Add the chocolate mixture and stir or beat everything until well combined.

Combine the flour with the baking powder, cinnamon and cloves and add to the batter in small amounts, beating after each addition. Now beat the egg whites until stiff ("stiff but not dry," as the old recipes say) and fold them in. Lastly, fold in the vanilla. Put the batter into 3 well-buttered 8-inch cake pans. Bake at 375° F for 30 minutes. Cool, then frost and fill with Buttercream Frosting (pages 170 to 171).

Pineapple (or Other Fruit) Upside-down Cake

This is one of the standard desserts in most Midwestern households. It's pretty to look at, fun to make and a real pleasure to eat.

My grandmother always made it in a cast-iron skillet, but you could use a large cake pan instead. Also, she invariably made it with canned pineapple, but you could substitute any canned or even fresh fruit (for instance, apples, pears or peaches). Just be sure to drain the canned fruits well and peel and slice fresh fruits.

⅔ cup butter, divided
1 cup light or dark brown sugar
Sliced pineapple or other fruit (see above)
Maraschino cherries and/or whole walnuts or pecans (optional)

FOR THE BATTER

1½ cups flour
2 teaspoons baking powder
⅛ teaspoon salt
¾ cup granulated sugar
1 egg, lightly beaten
⅔ cup milk
1 teaspoon vanilla
Whipped cream (optional)

Melt ⅓ cup of the butter in a large cast-iron skillet or cake pan. Sprinkle the brown sugar on evenly, then arrange the fruit and, if you're using them, the nuts in an attractive pattern. For the classic Pineapple Upside-Down Cake, use pineapple slices, with a maraschino cherry in the center of each one.

To make the batter: Combine the flour, baking powder, salt and sugar in a mixing bowl. Melt the remaining ⅓ cup butter. Mix it with the egg, milk and vanilla and stir this mixture into the dry ingredients.

Pour the batter over the brown sugar and fruit in the pan. Bake at 350° F for 50 minutes, then invert immediately onto a large plate. Serve at room temperature, perhaps topped with a little whipped cream.

Buttercream Frosting

This is the favorite frosting of many people who live, cook and eat in the heartland. It tastes a lot like hard sauce—in fact, that's what it is, just a vanilla hard sauce, made thinner than usual. Make it by hand, with a mixer or in a food processor.

½ cup (1 stick) butter
1 pound (or less) confectioners' sugar
1 teaspoon pure vanilla (or more, to taste)
About 2 tablespoons milk or light cream

Start out by creaming the butter with about half of the sugar. Now start adding the liquids in very small amounts, just a drop or 2 at a time, alternately with heaping spoonfuls of the sugar. Add the vanilla first, so you'll be sure to get it all in. Don't feel you have to use all the sugar—stop when you have a lovely, soft, creamy frosting.

Fluffy White Frosting

This is the dress-up frosting, the one Midwesterners use when they want to create a spectacular cake. There are a number of names for frostings of this sort—White Mountain, Seven-Minute and so on—but they all have the same effect: fluff.

My aversion to making these frostings (or icings—same thing) goes back to the day I helped my mother make a so-called Seven-Minute Icing which took a full forty-five minutes to beat, even with an electric beater. However, they are needed in a Midwestern cook's bag of tricks, and are a necessity for my favorite cake (Mint-Chocolate Shadow Cake, page 167). This is one of the better and more dependable versions.

2 cups sugar
2 tablespoons light corn syrup
1 cup water
2 egg whites
1/8 teaspoon salt
1/8 teaspoon cream of tartar
1 teaspoon vanilla

Bring the sugar, corn syrup and water to a boil in a medium-size saucepan, stirring occasionally until the sugar is dissolved. Boil until the mixture reaches 238° F on a candy thermometer (the thread or soft-ball stage).

Beat the egg whites and the salt with a mixer until they are frothy. Now add the boiling sugar syrup in a thin stream, keeping the mixer going constantly. Keep beating until the icing begins to thicken and seems spreadable, then beat in first the cream of tartar, then the vanilla.

Lemon Icebox Cake

Icebox cakes are not baked (although they do sometimes have a cooked filling). They're assembled, then chilled, so they're perfect for summer days because they don't heat up the kitchen—not to mention the fact that they make a showy and delicious dessert. They seem to be derived from English trifles, but are never called by that name.

36 ladyfingers, split
1 cup sugar
Grated rind of 1 lemon
½ cup (1 stick) butter, beaten until soft
4 eggs, divided
3 tablespoons lemon juice

Line the bottom and sides of a springform pan with ladyfingers, rounded sides toward the pan. Cut if needed to make them fit. (Don't use them all as yet.)

Now combine the sugar and lemon peel and add gradually to the butter in a large bowl. Beat the egg yolks in one by one, then beat in the lemon juice. Whip the egg whites until stiff and fold them into the lemon mixture.

Put a layer of this filling in the springform pan, then a layer of ladyfingers. Repeat this layering until the pan is full, ending with ladyfingers, arranged like the spokes of a wheel, on top. Chill until very firm (at least 8 hours). To serve, remove the outer part of the springform pan, leaving the cake on the base. • *SERVES 6 to 8.*

Chocolate Icebox Cake

Icebox cakes, because they elicited such raves when they were served, turned up often at meetings of the many clubs to which the women of most Midwestern small towns used to belong. In Mount Pleasant, there were several bridge clubs plus special ones such as the Art Study Club and the one known as Wednesday Club.

Wednesday Club terrified me, since it was made up of the grandes dames of the town. I particularly remember one meeting when I was in my early teens. It was the custom to bring a "current event" to Wednesday Club. You'd read aloud or tell about some news item. My grandmother thought I'd be forgiven for not having one ready, but our hostess said, "Glennie, dear, there's an article about your Uncle Tom in the new Reader's Digest, and I'd like you to read it to us. I'm sure it's very interesting."

Well, I'd seen the article. It was about what my uncle was doing in those days—directing the army's attempts to stamp out venereal disease. It mentioned some rather unspeakable things. Interesting was no word for it. There was no way I could read it to those nice ladies—and no way I could get out of reading it. They insisted. So for what seemed like hours, I stumbled and skimmed my way through the article, trying desperately to find parts of it that wouldn't shock the ladies. It was agony.

Later, though, my grandmother said to me, "Don't worry, dear. They all know a great deal more about these things than you do." And, of course, she was absolutely right, though it was hard to believe it then.

36 ladyfingers, split
9 ounces German's sweet
   chocolate
5 eggs, separated
4 tablespoons water
4 tablespoons sugar
1 cup heavy cream
2 tablespoons confectioners' sugar

First, line a bowl with waxed paper. The easiest way: Use overlapping 3-inch strips.

Cover this with a layer of ladyfingers, rounded sides toward the bowl.

Melt the chocolate over very low heat (or use a double boiler). Beat the egg yolks and water together; add to the chocolate along with the sugar. Stir for the few minutes required to cook the mixture until thick. Remove from the heat and allow to cool, then beat the egg whites until stiff and fold in. Assemble in the bowl in layers with the remaining ladyfingers. Chill at least 4 hours.

To serve, turn out onto a serving plate. Remove the waxed paper. Whip the cream; fold in the confectioners' sugar; use this to cover the top of the cake.

• *SERVES 6 to 8.*

Puddings,

Ice Cream,

Cookies

and Other Desserts

7 he previous chapter, Pies and Cakes, contains most of the Midwestern desserts which are considered fancy. Puddings, ice cream, cookies, fruit desserts and such, which you'll find in this chapter, are totally delicious but are considered more everyday family fare. (Believe me, though, you can delight a dinner party with most of them.)

Chocolate Bread Pudding with Hard Sauce

The Midwest seems to produce more than its share of chocoholics. Many members of my family fall into this category, and I do, too.

Any of the chocolate recipes in this book will do nicely to assuage a craving, but for many people in the heartland, chocolate bread pudding is number one. The Hard Sauce (see page 189) is an important part of the recipe. You serve the pudding hot, and the cold sauce melts into fabulous pools of flavor on it.

3 ounces unsweetened chocolate
1 cup sugar
4 cups milk
2 tablespoons butter
1 teaspoon pure vanilla
2 cups bread cubes

Put the chocolate, sugar and milk in a saucepan and heat, stirring often, until the chocolate is melted. Add the butter, vanilla and bread cubes and stir gently until the butter has melted. Pour into a greased pan and bake at 350° F for 1 hour. • *SERVE very hot to 4 with Hard Sauce (see page 189).*

The Creamiest Rice Pudding

There are many good versions of rice pudding in the Midwest, but this one's the creamiest—and therefore the best, to my way of thinking.

4 cups milk
½ cup rice
½ cup sugar
2 eggs
1 teaspoon real vanilla
¼ teaspoon cinnamon

Combine the milk, rice and sugar in a heavy saucepan (or double boiler). Cook over low heat (or over simmering water), stirring occasionally, until the rice is tender and has absorbed almost all the liquid. This will take about 1 hour. Remove from the heat.

Now beat the eggs lightly in a medium-size bowl. Add a large spoonful (about ¼ cup) of the rice mixture and mix well, then stir this combination into the rest of the rice along with the vanilla. Spoon the pudding into a serving dish, sprinkle on the cinnamon and chill well.
• *SERVES 4.*

Mississippi Valley Bread Pudding with Raisins

This is a gorgeous pudding. Serve it warm or at room temperature—or even cold for breakfast the next day.

1 large loaf white bread (1 pound or a bit more)
3 eggs, beaten
1¼ cups white sugar
¼ cup light brown sugar
1 small can evaporated milk
1 tablespoon pure vanilla
½ teaspoon nutmeg
1 cup raisins

Tear the bread into fairly small pieces. Put in a bowl, cover with water and let sit for just a minute or 2. Squeeze out the water, then add all the other ingredients to the soggy bread. Pour into a buttered 8 × 11-inch pan and bake at 350° F until puffed and brown. • *SERVE with hard sauce (page 189) to 4 to 8.*

Apple Crisp

Apple Crisp is one of the most pleasant desserts in all the heartland. It's part smooth and part, well, crisp, *and the flavor is just a little spicy. To me, this is the best thing to be done with the apples that are Johnny Appleseed's heritage, though the Old-Fashioned Apple Pie on page 157 is a close second, and I sometimes think I prefer Apple Crisp with Oatmeal Topping, below. (I share a common Midwestern trait of thinking that something good I've just eaten is the best food in the world. I don't think there's a single dish in either of these dessert chapters that I haven't felt this way about at one time or another.)*

> 6 tart apples, peeled, cored and thickly sliced
> 2 tablespoons water
> 2 tablespoons white sugar
> ¼ teaspoon cinnamon
> 1 cup flour
> ¼ cup light or dark brown sugar
> ½ cup butter
> Heavy cream, whipped or plain

Put the slices of apple in a buttered 8 × 12-inch pan. Sprinkle on the water. Mix the granulated sugar with the cinnamon and sprinkle this on next. Now combine the flour, brown sugar and butter, using your choice of a fork, your fingertips or a food processor. (My recommendation? Use your fingers.)

Pat this topping over the apples, pressing it down well. Bake at 375° F for 30 minutes, or until the apples are soft. Serve with cream, whipped or not. • *SERVES 6.*

APPLE CRISP WITH OATMEAL TOPPING

As I said above, sometimes this seems like a better Apple Crisp than the nonoatmeal recipe. The fact is that they're both just wonderful. At any rate, this version adds the pleasant flavor of oatmeal—and it's easier to convince yourself and others that it's a proper food for breakfast when it contains what is undoubtedly the heartland's favorite cereal.

To make Apple Crisp with Oatmeal Topping, just follow the recipe above for Apple Crisp, but substitute ¾ cup of oatmeal for ¾ cup of the flour.

Lemon Sponge Custard

It's easy to eat lots of this lovely, refreshing pudding. I had two helpings when Thelma Henson, who acquired the recipe when she lived in Michigan, served it to me, and I yearned for more. There's something about the flavor of fresh lemons and their grated peel that's irresistible and makes you feel that you're not eating very much. This is an illusion—but such a happy one.

- 2 tablespoons butter (plus more for greasing the custard cups)
- 1 cup sugar
- 2 tablespoons flour
- Dash of salt
- 1 cup hot milk
- 2 eggs, divided
- Juice and grated rind of 1 large lemon

Cream the butter and sugar and beat in the flour, salt, milk and egg yolks. Now beat the egg whites until stiff and add to the mixture along with the lemon juice and grated rind.

Put into 6 well-buttered 6-ounce custard cups. Place these in a pan of warm water and bake at 325° F for 45 minutes to 1 hour, or until very lightly browned. (There will be a sponge layer at the top of the cups and a sauce at the bottom.)
- *SERVES 3 to 6.*

Billy Sundae

Half the fun of reading Midwestern community cookbooks is seeing the delightful names given to many of the recipes. For instance, I recently came across a pudding called "The Next Best Thing to Robert Redford." Another book contains "Clean Stove Pork Chops." One of my favorites is "Billy Sundae," a play on the name of a popular revival minister of long ago. The original version of this comes from The Swedesburg Cook Book, *put out in the 1930s by the ladies of the Lutheran Church of Swedesburg, a very small town in southeastern Iowa. I've taken a few liberties with the recipe, but the effect is the same.*

- ¼ cup quick-cooking tapioca
- 1½ cups water
- ¼ cup white sugar
- ¼ light or dark brown sugar
- ½ cup chopped dates
- ½ cup broken nut meats (pecans or walnuts)
- 2 tablespoons butter, melted
- 1 teaspoon vanilla
- Heavy cream, whipped cream or vanilla ice cream for serving

Soak the tapioca in the water for half an hour. Then add the rest of the ingredients. Put into a well-buttered 2-quart baking dish and cook at 350° F for 1 hour. Serve hot, cold or at room temperature, topped with heavy cream, whipped cream or vanilla ice cream. • *SERVES 4.*

Strawberry Shortcake

This couldn't be a cookbook truly representative of Midwestern cooking unless it contained THE favorite dessert of the area—Strawberry Shortcake.

People in other parts of the country may use sponge cake as the base of their shortcake, but this is a heresy that would not be condoned in the heartland. My own disappointment when I see Strawberry Shortcake on a menu and find out it's made with cake is extreme and I order something else. (This, of course, could only happen in the East or possibly the Far West.)

1 batch Cream Biscuit dough
  (page 148)
2 tablespoons soft butter (optional)
1 quart strawberries
½ cup sugar
½ cup heavy cream, whipped

Roll the biscuit dough out about ½ inch thick and cut out 6 3-inch biscuits. Bake on an ungreased pan at 450° F for 10 to 15 minutes, or until light brown. Split each biscuit in half. Spread the insides with butter, if you wish. My grandmother didn't, so I don't.

Slice the strawberries, reserving a few whole ones for garnish, and combine gently with the sugar in a bowl. Refrigerate until dessert time.

Now put half of each biscuit on a plate. Top with a liberal amount of the strawberries and the juice that will have formed. Put the top of each biscuit in place and add more

of the strawberries. Now put on some of the whipped cream and top each creation with a whole strawberry. • *SERVES 6.*

If you want to make shortcake at a time of year when sweet berries aren't available, you can cheat by using frozen sliced, sweetened berries, thawed.

Graham Cracker Roll

Graham Cracker Roll is delicious! This is from a recipe handwritten more than fifty years ago by a good Midwestern cook. It didn't take much work to make even back in those days. Today, with a food processor, it practically makes itself.

"Put 1 pound Graham crackers, 12 ounces pitted dates, ½ pound marshmallows and ½ cup pecans through a food grinder." (Use a food processor.) "Add enough cream to make the mixture stick together and knead. Shape into a roll and put into refrigerator. Serve sliced, with whipped cream."
• *SERVES 4.*

Ozark Pudding

While it's generally believed that Ozark Pudding originated in the hill country of Arkansas, it's also well loved in other parts of the Ozarks. In a slightly different version, it's said to have been a favorite dish of Bess Truman (Mrs. Harry S.), the pride of Missouri.

1 egg
¾ cup sugar
¾ cup flour
1½ teaspoons baking powder
1½ teaspoons vanilla
¾ cup chopped apples
½ chopped pecans
Whipped cream

Beat the egg and sugar together, then beat in a combination of the flour and baking powder. Next, stir in the vanilla and chopped apples and pecans. Place in a buttered 8 × 8-inch pan, patting down to level. Bake at 350° F for 30 minutes, or until a nice light brown crust has formed. Serve warm, topped with whipped cream.
• *SERVES 4 to 6.*

Real Vanilla Ice Cream

You can't buy ice cream like this. I can say that with some assurance, since I spent decades looking for it. It's what was sometimes called "New York" ice cream in the Midwest when I was growing up. It had a deep, yellowish color and tasted strongly and richly of vanilla. Something similar was called "frozen custard," but bore no resemblance to the frozen custard of today's roadside stands. Finally, to the relief of my husband and children (who were growing tired of our having to turn the car around every time we passed a sign that said "frozen custard"), I learned how to make it. To my amusement, it turned out to actually be a frozen custard.

6 egg yolks
¾ cup sugar
2 cups milk
Pinch of salt
2 cups heavy cream
2 tablespoons pure vanilla

Mix the egg yolks, sugar, milk and salt together, preferably in a blender, then cook over very low heat or in a double boiler, stirring most of the time, until thickened enough to coat a spoon. (If it curdles a little, don't worry; it will uncurdle as it freezes.) Chill thoroughly, then add the heavy cream and the vanilla. Freeze in an ice cream maker—a hand-cranked one if you're really out to recreate the past or an electric one if you have other things to do with the rest of the day. • *MAKES a little less than 2 quarts.*

Chocolate Ice Cream

The ice cream that came out of the hand-cranked freezer on Midwestern picnics was and is most often chocolate—deep, luscious chocolate, with no namby-pambyness about it.

Follow the instructions above for Real Vanilla Ice Cream, but cut the vanilla down to 1 tablespoon and add 3 ounces of semisweet chocolate, melted, to the milk mixture before chilling.

Chocolate Chip Ice Cream

This is what Dorothy Macmillan, a family friend who was also a nurse, brought me every day of the six winter weeks she took care of me when I had pneumonia and was ensconced in a hospital bed in my grandparents' dining room. With medicine like this, who would want to get well?

Make Real Vanilla Ice Cream, but add 2 cups or a bit more of chipped semisweet chocolate. Don't use the chocolate bits you see in Toll House cookies, but don't chip the chocolate *too* fine, either.

And then there's chocolate chocolate chip. It's not notably Midwestern, but it certainly is good. Just add chipped chocolate to the chocolate ice cream mixture.

Strawberry or Peach Ice Cream

The essence of Midwestern summers. As you eat it, picture yourself gently going back and forth in a porch swing on a hot afternoon when the "snowball bushes" and the tea roses are in bloom.

Cut strawberries or peeled peaches into smallish bite-size pieces—3 cups of them. Toss the fruit with ½ cup sugar and refrigerate until the sugar is dissolved in the fruit's juices. Puree 2 cups of this in a blender or processor and add to the Real Vanilla Ice Cream mixture made with only ½ cup sugar and 2 teaspoons vanilla. Freeze, then stir in the remaining fruit pieces and their juice.

Ambrosia

When I was a child, Ambrosia was considered an everyday dessert, although a favorite one. But when my father was a little boy in Missouri in the first years of this century, it would have been an almost unheard-of luxury. Oranges were rare and expensive treats, and my father and his brothers and sisters were excited if they found one in their Christmas stockings. Because of this, I've always put an orange in my own children's stockings. Once in a while there's been a complaint from a child who felt the orange took up room that could be put to better use by an extra present or two, but I've kept up the tradition. I like the symbolism of the Christmas orange, a reminder in the midst of today's orgy of Christmas presents of the beauty of simple things and of how lucky we are.

Cut 6 navel oranges in half and scoop out the sections. Combine in a bowl with 1 cup of shredded or flaked coconut. Chill well, stirring occasionally. Serve in individual bowls, complete with the lovely juice that forms. • *SERVES 4 to 6.*

Ottumwa Apple Fritters with Cinnamon Sauce

We had relatives who lived in the town of Ottumwa, so part of every summer I spent in Iowa was a daylong visit to them. We were greeted with hugs, kisses and lots and lots of food. (And, of course, quite a bit of talk about how much I'd grown.) Of what they served us, I especially remember these apple fritters with cinnamon sauce, which were fabulous.

FOR THE FRITTERS

1 cup flour
1 teaspoon baking powder
¼ teaspoon salt
1 teaspoon sugar
1 egg, slightly beaten
⅔ cup milk
1 teaspoon butter, melted
1 cup finely minced apple
Oil for deep-frying

FOR THE SAUCE

½ cup sugar
1½ tablespoons cornstarch
½ teaspoon cinnamon
⅛ teaspoon nutmeg
⅞ cup water
2 tablespoons cider vinegar
2 tablespoons butter

To make the fritters: Combine the flour, baking powder, salt and sugar in a medium-size bowl. Beat the egg, milk and butter together briefly and stir into the dry ingredients. Add the minced apple. Drop by spoonfuls into the oil, which has been heated to 375° F, frying just a few fritters at a time to avoid crowding and lowering the heat too much. Turn each fritter once to brown nicely on both sides, then drain them on paper towels while you make the next batch.

To make the sauce: Combine the sugar, cornstarch, cinnamon and nutmeg in a fairly small saucepan. Add the water and cider vinegar and cook and stir over medium heat until thickened. Put in the butter and stir until melted. Serve warm or at room temperature. • *SERVES 4 to 6.*

Meringue Kisses

When I was about ten, I had a terribly hard time saying good-bye at the end of the summer when my grandmother put me on the train (the glamorous Burlington Zephyr, said to travel at seventy miles an hour) to start me on the way home.

It wasn't just that I hated to leave. I was also convinced that my grandmother was so old that she'd die before I could ever see her again. Of course, I didn't tell my grandmother about my fear, but Peggy Hoaglin, an old friend of the family, knew of my unhappiness and brought me a big box full of Meringue Kisses to eat on the train. It was an excellent idea. I nibbled and nibbled and gradually felt better, and to this day Meringue Kisses seem to me to be a very soothing food.

And I'm glad to say that my grandmother lived a good thirty or so years more.

  2 egg whites
  Large pinch of salt
  1 cup sugar
  ½ teaspoon vanilla

Beat the egg whites with the salt until stiff but not dry, then very gradually beat in first the sugar, then the vanilla.

Drop from a spoon, making little mounds, onto a buttered and floured tin and bake at 275° F for 20 minutes, or until they're firm and just barely colored. Remove from the pan while still warm. • *MAKES about 18 to 20 kisses—(enough to last all the way to Chicago on the Burlington Zephyr).*

Suzanne's Fudge Bars

Suzanne Dickson, my very dear godmother, still lives in Mount Pleasant, Iowa. She has disowned her fudge bars, but I think that's just modesty. They're in between brownies and fudge—moist, soft, intensely chocolaty. She taught me how to make them one summer afternoon in the big kitchen of her lovely white-washed brick house, with the sun streaming in, sheep outside in the fields, and warmth, peace and love surrounding us. She wrote me once that the success of the bars was probably that I remember them and her kitchen with nostalgia. That's no doubt part of it, but even without a memory like that, you're going to like her fudge bars.

  4 ounces unsweetened chocolate
  5 ounces (1 ¼ sticks) butter
  2 eggs
  ½ teaspoon pure vanilla
  2 cups sugar
  1 cup flour

Melt the chocolate and butter together in a medium-size saucepan. Cool, then add the eggs and vanilla. Combine the flour and sugar and gradually add them to the chocolate mixture. Pat the dough out about ½ inch thick in a small buttered pan and bake at 350° F for 15 minutes, or until the top is crusty and the insides still soft. Cut into bars while warm, but don't serve until cool. • *SERVES 4 to 6.*

Butterscotch Refrigerator Cookies

High on the list of favorite treats when I was growing up in the Midwest were my mother's Butterscotch Refrigerator Cookies. To make these, she'd form a cookie dough into rolls and keep it in the refrigerator. Then, whenever the occasion arose (when a small daughter pleaded, for instance), she would slice off some cookies and bake them. (The small daughter was very grateful.)

You can buy rolls of cookie dough of this sort in the dairy section of supermarkets these days, but the top cooks in the heartland still make their own—not just because they want to save money (though this does often come into it) but also because the homemade cookies are much better.

1 cup (2 sticks) butter
1½ cups light brown sugar
2 eggs
1 teaspoon pure vanilla
3 cups flour, sifted (or presifted)
¼ teaspoon salt
½ cup broken pecans or walnuts
   (optional)

Cream the butter and sugar until light and fluffy, then beat in the eggs and vanilla. Mix the flour and salt together, then stir in, along with the nuts, if you're using them, to make a fairly stiff dough. Form this into 3 or 4 rolls, each about 2 inches in diameter. Wrap in waxed paper and keep in the refrigerator until needed. (Chill the rolls at least 2 hours before baking.)

When you want some cookies, unwrap a roll of dough and cut off as many as you need, slicing them about ¼ inch thick. Place on a greased baking sheet and bake at 400° F for 10 minutes, or until light tan.

• *MAKES about 6 dozen cookies.*

Pinwheel Cookies

One of my earliest memories is of sitting on a stool in our kitchen in Winnetka, Illinois, and watching the making of Pinwheel Cookies. I remember there was a white dough and a chocolate dough and that these were put together, chilled a bit, then cut and baked—and that the result was a cookie so pretty it seemed downright miraculous to me. (It still does.)

To make Pinwheel Cookies, first make the dough for Butterscotch Refrigerator Cookies, above, but use 1½ cups white sugar instead of brown and omit the nuts. Divide the dough into 2 parts. To one half, add 1 square (1 ounce) melted unsweetened baking chocolate. Chill. Now roll the white dough and the chocolate dough separately between sheets of waxed paper until each is about ¼ inch thick and 3½ inches wide. Place the chocolate dough on top of the white dough and roll the 2 together tightly, like a jelly roll. Wrap in waxed paper and chill before slicing.

Bake, sliced, on a greased baking sheet at 375° F for about 12 minutes, or until just set—you don't want the white layer to darken. • *MAKES about 6 dozen beautiful little pinwheels.*

Radio Cookies

The mother of a friend of mine told me this story:

When she was a brand-new bride (in the mid-1920s, I think), she used to listen to one of the first clear-channel radio stations as she did her housework. Every day, she'd write down the recipes given on the station's cooking show and cook that night's dinner accordingly.

One day her husband told one of his coworkers about the excellent dinner his wife had cooked the night before. "That's funny," the other worker said. "I had exactly the same dinner myself." It turned out that everyone else in the office had eaten the same meal the previous night and had, in fact, been eating identical meals for weeks. All their wives had been listening to the radio and following its instructions!

Radio Cookies, which turned up in a Midwestern community cookbook from that era, must have come from the same source. Here's the recipe, exactly as it appeared:

"One cup lard, 1 cup sugar, 1 egg, 1 cup sweet milk, 1 level teaspoon soda, ¼ teaspoon nutmeg, enough flour to stiffen and roll. Cut in strips or squares. Bake in moderate oven. Sprinkle sugar over top."

Dutch Santa Claus Cookies

On our yearly summer excursions to Des Moines, the state capital, we always stopped at Pella, Iowa, to buy some wonderful Dutch cookies.

Joan Kuyper Farver, chairman of the board of the Rolscreen Company, manufacturer of Pella windows and doors, has been a great help in my quest to learn more about Pella, sending me brochures, letters and recipes. She wrote, "Pella is well known for its Dutch treats and customs which reflect the pride we have in our Dutch heritage."

The ideal time these days to go to Pella is in May, during the annual Tulip Time festival. Then you'll see hundreds of the residents dressed in authentic Dutch costumes and be able to watch such interesting events as the ritual street scrubbing, which precedes the colorful Volks Parade with its bands and lighted floats.

At any time of year, though, you can visit the Historical Village and see Wyatt Earp's boyhood home and the famous Klokkenspel with its carillon and parading mechanical figures. And all year long, you can stop at one of several bakeries and pick up the Dutch cookies of my childhood. Mrs. Farver has sent me recipes for two of these cookies— St. Nikolas Koekjes (or Santa Claus Cookies) and Dutch Letters (Banket Gebak). Try them both and you, too, will come under the spell of Pella, the "City of Refuge."

First, Santa Claus Cookies, about which Mrs. Farver says, "These are a traditional favorite year-round, not just at Christmas, as the name might imply. In fact, the bakery offers them in three sizes and a variety of molded shapes."

1½ cups (3 sticks) butter
2 cups light or dark brown sugar
3½ cups flour
1 teaspoon cinnamon
½ teaspoon nutmeg
½ teaspoon ground cloves
1 teaspoon baking powder
1 egg, beaten
1 scant teaspoon salt

Cream the butter and sugar and add the remaining ingredients. This makes a very stiff dough. Mold the cookies on a Santa Claus cookie board (you can buy these in Pella) or form into rolls as for refrigerator cookies and slice when well chilled, after about 2 hours. Bake for 10 to 12 minutes at 350° F.

Dutch Letters

These almond paste cookies are usually made in the shape of an S these days, though Pella bakeries will make them in the shape of any letter you wish. When you make them at home, it's fun to shape them in the initials of yourself and/or anyone you'll be serving them to.

I credit my lifelong love for marzipan to early ingestion of these cookies.

    1 pound almond paste
    2 cups sugar
    3 eggs, lightly beaten
    4 cups flour
    2 cups butter or other shortening
    1 cup ice water
    ¼ cup milk

Combine the almond paste, sugar and eggs in a bowl and set aside. Now make a pastry dough: Combine the flour with the butter or other shortening, then add the water a few tablespoons at a time, using only enough to make a firm dough. Chill for at least 1 hour.

Now divide the pastry dough into 4 parts and roll each on a floured board into a 13 × 8-inch rectangle. Cut these in half to make 8 13 × 4-inch strips.

Form the almond mixture into 8 rolls, each 12 inches long and the diameter of a dime. Place one roll on each strip of dough. Fold over first the ends and then the sides, moistening one edge to seal before pressing closed. Shape into letters or bake them straight and cut them after they're cooked.

Whatever you decide, place the rolls, seam side down, on baking sheets. Brush the tops with milk. Bake at 425° F for 10 minutes, then prick holes on the top of each and bake at 375° F for another 10 minutes, or until lightly browned.

Hard Sauce

Don't use brandy or rum or liqueurs in the hard sauce. Those are Eastern touches. Midwestern hard sauce uses pure vanilla and is unbeatable.

    4 tablespoons butter
    1 cup confectioners' sugar
    1 teaspoon pure vanilla
    A few drops of water or milk

Soften the butter by beating it well in a mixer, food processor or by hand. Add the sugar, a tablespoon or so at a time, alternately with a drop or 2 of vanilla. When you've added all the vanilla, switch to water or milk. Stop when you have a moderately soft sauce. (It will thicken as it becomes cold.) Chill for at least 1 or 2 hours.
• *MAKES 1 cup.*

Chocolate Butter

Back when we all lived outside of Chicago, my parents used to see a lot of Bud and Georgiana ("Georgie") Gibson—and did me the favor of making them my godparents. One night, after I had gone to bed, I heard them all laughing and exclaiming down in the kitchen. How I wanted to be down there, too! Then dear Bud brought me some of what all the carrying-on was about: Chocolate Butter on an English muffin. I don't think I'd ever eaten anything as good.

- ¼ cup cocoa powder
- ½ cup sugar
- Water
- ½ cup (1 stick) butter, at room temperature or softened

Combine the cocoa and sugar in a small bowl, then add water, a few drops at a time, until the mixture becomes the consistency of mud. Stir in the butter.

As I write this, I'm eating an English muffin with Chocolate Butter and watching Bud and Georgie's son, Charles Gibson, co-host of *Good Morning America*. Charlie's an Easterner now, but his friendliness and candor show his Midwestern heritage.

Mary's Chocolate Sauce

Thursday evenings were band concert nights in Mount Pleasant, Iowa, when I used to spend summers with my grandparents there. The concerts were held in a Victorian bandstand in the parklike square that formed the heart of the town. The music was, I suppose, pretty terrible, but we all enjoyed it. Every Sousa march was blared out, along with such gems as "The Skaters' Waltz." The system was for most of the listeners to sit in their cars, which were parked around the square, and for the car horns to be tooted to signify applause. I think the people in the cars tried to outdo each other, as the noise of the horns was deafening.

We always parked in one particular spot, right across from the Princess Candy Kitchen, so we could have a sundae there as soon as the band concert was over. The Candy Kitchen seemed like paradise to me. There were booths upholstered in shiny red plastic and remote controls for the jukebox—and bliss-producing things to eat.

You could get grilled cheese and other sandwiches at the Candy Kitchen, and milkshakes so thick they had to be eaten with a spoon, but the three of us always ordered sundaes. The ice cream could vary (though vanilla was the usual choice), but the sauce was always chocolate, and the sundae was, of course, topped with real whipped cream, walnuts and a maraschino cherry. You can imagine how much I looked forward to Thursday evenings!

My Aunt Mary, who grew up in Lacon, Illinois, gave us her recipe for a chocolate sauce that was even better than the one at the Candy Kitchen:

⅓ cup butter
1½ ounces unsweetened baking chocolate
1 cup confectioners' sugar
1 cup heavy cream
2 teaspoons pure vanilla

Combine all the ingredients in the top of a double boiler and cook over simmering water, stirring often, until the sauce is almost as thick as you want it to be. (It will thicken more as it cools.) Keep refrigerated, then use either cold or rewarmed.
• *MAKES 1¾ cups.*

The Bountiful Pantry

A pantry is a little room lined with shelves designed to hold row after row of jelly glasses and Mason jars full of the preserved or home-canned fruits or vegetables of the summer garden. For many families in the old days, a full pantry meant survival through the long, barren winter. The advent of the home freezer, however, brought a quick end to the home canning of most vegetables. Why should a person home can peas, green beans and such when freezing was easier, just as inexpensive, and often produced better results?

Nothing, though, could replace homemade jellies, jams, relishes and condiments, so the idea of the pantry has continued to flourish. Women (and some men, too) still squirrel away neatly labeled glass jars full of summer's goodness. Those who don't have actual pantries use kitchen cupboards or, more likely, open shelves or windowsills where everyone can see and admire the sparkling colors, the reds, yellows, oranges, ambers, greens and purples.

The recipes in this chapter are just a few examples of what can go into the bountiful pantry. They're chosen to represent things you either can't buy at all in stores or would have to pay a fortune for—and they're all foods Midwesterners love and use on an almost daily basis.

Some of the recipes call for a jelly bag, which you may well not have. They're available in many fancy kitchen stores or by mail order, or you can improvise one by lining a colander with flannel or several thicknesses of cheesecloth. Put the colander over a pot; pour in the prepared fruit; gather up the edges of the cloth and tie securely with a long piece of string. Loop this over a hook or cabinet knob so the weight of the fruit will force the juice out into the pot below. (Don't try to help this process by squeezing the bag or you will suffer the sad fate of having cloudy jelly.) Ideally, let the fruit drip through the bag overnight, though you can get by with just 3 or 4 hours. (So you end up with a spoonful or two less jelly. . . .)

Old-time preserves and jellies went into glasses that had to be sealed with melted paraffin. Today it's best to use Mason jars with special lids that give a perfect seal. These jars come in several sizes. According to the latest thinking, you should process the filled jars in a hot water bath. (Use a special canner or a deep pot with a rack. Put the jars into the pot, add enough boiling water to come 2 inches above the jars and boil for 15 minutes or according to the instructions that come with the jars.)

The sheeting stage mentioned in most jelly recipes is hard to describe, but unmistakable once you know what to look for. You start as soon as the juices come to a boil by dipping a large metal spoon in the pot and holding it sideways so you can see the runoff. You will have reached the stage you want when the mixture has thickened enough so, instead of coming off the spoon in a stream, the juices run together and come off in a sheet.

Pickled Peaches

Pickled Peaches come under the heading of necessities for the Midwestern pantry. They have to be on hand to garnish roasts and add their marvelous piquancy to just about any sort of meal. They're also considered a real treat when served with cottage cheese and Boiled Dressing (see page 133) as a salad. They're served cold, or at least cool—at cellar or "cold pantry" temperature.

    7 pounds smallish peaches,
        preferably clingstone
    3 cups cider vinegar
    3 cups water
    6 cups sugar
    3 sticks cinnamon, broken up
    1½ tablespoons whole cloves

First, remove the peach skins by pouring on boiling water, then peeling. (Don't skip this step. I did once, and was very sorry.) Then bring the cider vinegar, water, sugar and spices to a boil in a large pot. Boil for 5 minutes, then add the peaches—carefully, so they don't splash—and simmer until they are tender. Put the peaches into freshly sterilized jars. Fill the jars with the syrup, dividing the spices equally, then seal (see page 194). • *MAKES about 10 pints.*

If you haven't planned ahead and gotten to work in pickling season, see the next recipe. You can still have your Pickled Peaches, even at the last moment.

Emergency Pickled Peaches

Community and church cookbooks from the Midwest abound in emergency recipes for this and for that. Emergency usually translates into "quick." In the case of pickled peaches, though, it also means that even though it's midwinter and you didn't manage to pickle your peaches when they were in season, there's still hope for you.

    1 1-pound can peach halves
    ½ cup sugar
    ⅓ cup cider vinegar
    1 tablespoon whole cloves
    1½ sticks cinnamon, broken up

Drain the juice from the peaches into a saucepan. Add the sugar, cider vinegar and spices. Boil gently for 15 minutes, then add the peaches. Turn off the heat, cover the pan and let it sit for 5 minutes, then pack the peaches into a sterilized jar or 2, dividing the spices and filling the jar with the syrup. Seal (see page 194) unless they're to be used in the next few days.

If you want to use your pickled peaches in the near future, just put them in your refrigerator, covered, for as long as a week or two. They're ready to use as soon as they're made.

Pickled Beets

Although there are plenty of people who start from scratch, boiling and peeling beets, some of the very nicest Pickled Beets start out as beets in a can. I'm not talking about the already pickled beets available on many supermarket shelves; they don't measure up at all. These are special, just right, and best of all, perhaps, because they're your very own. So don't feel guilty if you don't boil and peel fresh beets to pickle. You're in good company.

This amount is fairly small and not designed to be canned. It's to be used within a week or so, though I can't imagine it ever remaining uneaten that long.

1 ½ pounds tiny beets, boiled and
    peeled, or larger ones, boiled,
    peeled and sliced (or use
    1 28-ounce can very tiny beets or
    sliced beets)
⅓ cup sugar
⅓ cup cider vinegar

If you start with fresh beets, scrub them well and boil in a small amount of water. Use ¾ cup of their cooking juices (or drain the juice from canned beets and use that). Put into a saucepan with the sugar and cider vinegar and boil gently, uncovered for 10 minutes.

Pour this mixture over the beets. Let cool, then keep under refrigeration. • *MAKES about 3½ cups, including the liquid.*

Crisp Watermelon Pickles

All watermelon pickles, even the ones you can buy in grocery stores, are good to have on hand to add a little spice to a meal. You can't buy any, though, with the crispness of these. (Alum does the trick. Some old heartland recipes call for the use of slaked lime to produce crispness, but this is something I feel you shouldn't mess around with.)

Watermelon pickles, like the Corncob Jelly and Corncob Syrup later in this chapter, turn something (watermelon rind) that would normally be thrown away into an asset. Things like this gladden Midwestern hearts, mine among them. (It's hard to understand why grocery store watermelon pickles are so expensive, too.)

This recipe calls for the rind from a whole, large watermelon. If you have only a small amount of rind, it's still worthwhile turning it into pickles. Just cut the other ingredients down. And if you don't have any alum, that's all right, too. Your pickles just won't be as crisp; the flavor will be the same, and that's the main thing.

4 quarts peeled, trimmed-of-all-red-flesh and cut-up-into-small-squares watermelon rind (that's the rind from 1 large watermelon)
1 teaspoon alum
½ teaspoon salt
Water (see below for amount)
1 quart cider vinegar
4 pounds sugar
4 cinnamon sticks, broken
16 whole cloves
2 thinly sliced lemons

Put the prepared watermelon rind, the alum and the salt in a very large pot. Add enough water to cover. Boil until the rind is tender, about ½ hour. Drain thoroughly, then cool in ice-cold water. Drain again. When dry, divide the rind between 4 1-pint canning jars.

Now put the cider vinegar and sugar in a large pot along with 2 cups of water. Bring to a boil, then add the cinnamon sticks, cloves and lemon slices, all tied in a cheesecloth bag. Boil together until the syrup becomes clear, then remove the spice bag and divide the boiling syrup between the jars. (Most people discard the spices at this point, but I like the look of a piece of cinnamon stick and a couple of cloves in each jar, so I open the spice bag and add them.)

Seal the jars at once (see page 194) and try to refrain from using the pickles for about a month, when they'll be fully flavored.
• *MAKES about 4 1-pint jars.*

Red Pepper Relish

Red Pepper Relish, sometimes known as "Pepper Jam" or "Pepper Hash," goes well with any meat. I've been known to take some along to a restaurant when I plan to order hamburger and want it to taste really good. Combining the making of this with the Red Pepper Jelly below is my own idea, but that's just the Midwestern blood coming out in me. I couldn't stand seeing the pepper juice go to waste.

Many Midwesterners use half red peppers and half green. I don't because I want the jelly made from the juice to have a pretty color.

12 large sweet red peppers,
   deseeded
2 medium onions
2 teaspoons salt
2 cups sugar
2 cups cider vinegar

Grind the peppers and onions together (or use a food processor). Mix with the salt, then let the mixture sit for at least 4 hours. Drain off the juice that accumulates, pressing down on the vegetables (and saving the juice for the next recipe). Combine the vegetables with the sugar and cider vinegar and cook stirring often, until thick. Pack into freshly sterilized jelly glasses. Process in a hot water bath (see page 194).
• *MAKES 5 8-ounce glasses.*

Red Pepper Jelly

You can use this jelly the same way you would the relish above, to go with any sort of meat, or you can melt it to use for a sauce or glaze on chicken, roast pork or ham. It makes an interesting sandwich, too, combined with cream cheese.

Measure the drained juice left from making Red Pepper Relish, above. To this, add enough white vinegar to make a total of 2 cups of liquid. Now add a dash of Tabasco sauce and 4 cups of sugar. Bring to a full boil, then add ½ bottle of liquid pectin (Certo, that is). Boil for 1½ minutes. Ladle into freshly sterilized jelly glasses. Process in a hot water bath (see page 194).
• *MAKES 4 8-ounce glasses.*

Corncob Jelly

Here is yet another example of the fine heartland *"waste not, want not"* philosophy. Why should you throw away corncobs when they can be turned into a terrific jelly? (Or into Corncob Syrup, the following recipe.)

12 ears corn
2 quarts water
1 package powdered pectin (e.g., Sure-Jel)
3 cups sugar

Cut the kernels from the cobs and reserve for another dish. Break the cobs into smallish pieces and boil with the water for 30 minutes. Strain through cheesecloth or a fine-mesh sieve.

Mix 3 cups of this liquid with the Sure-Jel or other powdered pectin. Bring to a full boil, then add the sugar and boil for 5 minutes, or until it registers 222° F on a candy/jelly thermometer or reaches the sheeting stage. (See page 194.) Ladle into jelly glasses. Process in a hot water bath.
• *FILLS 3 8-ounce glasses.*

Corncob Syrup

Maple Syrup has always been a luxury, especially in the Midwest (although some is made there). You have to put <u>something</u> on your pancakes and waffles, though. Many (my father's family, for instance) used sorghum, a very heavy, excruciatingly sweet sugar by-product syrup, instead. Others used a sugar syrup mixed with maple flavoring. And, of course, large numbers bought Log Cabin syrup, Vermont Maid, and the like.

Best of all the substitutes was, and is, Corncob Syrup. In fact, there are those who prefer it to maple syrup because of its gentle taste of sweet corn.

Please read the comments about the previous recipe, Corncob Jelly. They all apply here as well.

12 ears corn
2 quarts water
2½ cups light brown sugar

Cut the kernels from the cobs and reserve for another dish. Break the cobs into smallish pieces and boil with the water for 40 to 45 minutes, or until the water is reduced by half. Strain through cheesecloth or a fine-mesh sieve.

Combine the 4 cups of liquid you now have with the brown sugar and cook over fairly low heat for 15 minutes, or until approximately as thick as Grade A maple syrup. Either pour into sterilized glasses and process in a hot water bath (see page 194) or just keep the syrup under refrigeration.
• *MAKES about 2 cups.*

Paradise Jelly

Most old home orchards in the Midwest contained two or three quince trees for making quince jam and quince jelly. Then, when cranberries began coming into the area with regularity (and when they began to be grown in Wisconsin), someone figured out this combination of three fruits. All I can say is that it is aptly named.

Today, quinces often turn up in the marketplace in the fall of the year, just when apples and cranberries are at their finest, too.

6 pounds juicy apples
3 pounds quinces
1 12-ounce package cranberries

First, read the jelly-making hints that begin on page 194.

If you're going to make Paradise Jam, the next recipe (and you really should), core the apples and quinces now. Otherwise, don't. In either case, cut them into quarters, removing the seeds as you go. (If the quinces are very large, cut them into pieces the same size as the apple quarters.)

Put the apple quarters and the cranberries in a large pan. Add water until the fruit is barely covered. Boil gently until the apples are very soft. Meanwhile, put the quinces in another pot. Barely cover them with water and boil gently until they, too, are very soft.

Next, let the contents of both pots drip together through a jelly bag. Save the pulp in the bag if you're being wise and making

Paradise Jam. Simmer the juices for 10 minutes to strengthen the flavor, then make the jelly, which traditional wisdom says has to be done in small batches. (I always make at least a double batch, though, and have encountered no problems.) For a single batch:

Put 4 cups of the juice in a large pot and add 4 cups of sugar. Boil until the sheeting stage is reached or a candy/jelly thermometer registers 222° F, skimming off the foam. Pour into sterilized jelly glasses and process in a hot water bath (see page 194). Continue until all the juice has been used. (Remember to save some for the making of Paradise Jam—better yet, see the note below.) • *Each batch cooks up into 4 8-ounce glasses.*

A tip that will help you with the logistics if you're going to make Paradise Jam: Before you make the jelly, prepare the pulp for jam, as described in the next recipe. Measure it, then reserve 1 cup of Paradise juice for every 3 cups of pulp.

Paradise Jam

Here we go again, turning something that would normally be thrown away into something wonderful. There are those, including my brother-in-law, Louis, who say this is the best jam in the world. I won't give them any argument.

First, read the jelly-making instructions that begin on page 194.

Paradise Jam is made in conjunction with Paradise Jelly. Go over the pulp that's left in the jelly bag, removing the apple and quince skins, then run the rest through a food mill.

As with Paradise Jelly, you're supposed to make small batches: To every 3 cups of fruit pulp, add 1 cup of juice and 4 cups of sugar. Cook over medium-high heat, stirring frequently and thoroughly, until the sheeting stage is reached or a candy/jelly thermometer reaches 222° F. Put into sterilized jelly glasses and process in a hot water bath (see page 194). • *Every batch makes 4 8-ounce glasses.*

Superior Apple Jelly

I said in the introduction to this chapter that I'd be giving you recipes for things that either couldn't be bought in stores or would cost a mint if you could find them. I've already made one exception, Pickled Beets, because they're so much better than the store-bought ones.

And here's apple jelly, which you can buy in every grocery store, and for not too much money, too. The thing is that apple jelly you make yourself is an entirely different thing from any you can buy. It's tender, fresh-tasting and absolutely glorious—well worth the small amount of effort involved.

The color and taste of your jelly depend on the sort of apple you use. Look for a tart apple with a red skin. First, read the jelly-making hints that begin on page 194.

Cut your apples into quarters. Put them in a large pot. Barely cover with water and boil until the apples fall apart. Pour the contents of the pot into a jelly bag and drain.

Now measure the juice and add an equal amount of sugar. Make small batches, using 4 cups each of juice and sugar, or cook all the jelly at once, using equal measures of juice and sugar. Boil until it reaches 222° F or passes the sheeting test. Pour into sterilized jelly glasses and process in a hot water bath.

I would tell you how to make the currant jelly my mother did, too, if I thought you could possibly have access to any currants. Sadly, they were thought to be carriers of the Dutch Elm Disease and were rooted up wherever they could be found. Mother had a secret currant bush patch, far away from any elms. Every year, she would have a jelly-making binge, doing it the way her mother had taught her in Iowa, and we'd have a yearlong supply of this ruby-red magic.

Strawberry-Rhubarb Jam

Winter in the Midwest is hard, long and cold. The contrast of spring, with its greenery, flowers and birds, is beautiful and exciting.

All winter long, the only fresh fruit available in the old days was that which had been home-canned or turned into jams and jellies. But come spring, two fruits appeared—rhubarb and strawberries. The two were eaten separately and together and made into this famous jam and also into pies and puddings. (Strawberry-Rhubarb Pie is on page 159.)

Today, even some very worldly Midwesterners who don't do much in the way of preserving and canning make Strawberry-Rhubarb Jam. It's one of nature's finest flavor combinations—and, simple though it is to make, it doesn't turn up on supermarket shelves.

It can be used as a meat or game accompaniment as well as a jam, and it's the handiest way you'll ever find to keep springtime in a jar.

6 cups rhubarb, cut into ½-inch
 lengths
6 cups crushed strawberries
8 cups sugar

First, read the jelly-making hints beginning on page 194.

Combine all the ingredients in a large saucepan and let sit for 1 hour or more to let the juices run out a bit. Now bring to a boil over medium heat and boil, stirring often, for about 20 minutes, or until thick and clear. Put into freshly sterilized jelly glasses and process in a hot water bath.
• *MAKES about 8 8-ounce jars.*

Tomato-Citrus Marmalade

The people who settled Nebraska, Kansas, Oklahoma and the Dakotas, spurred primarily by the Homestead Act of 1862 and the opening up of Oklahoma for homesteading in 1889, were tough, in the best sense of the word. They had to be. To begin with, their new land was basically treeless, which meant there was no wood available for house building or for cooking fires. Undaunted, they built houses of sod (sometimes known as "Nebraska marble") and cooked over "buffalo chips" and dried corncobs and stalks.

Some had trouble with the Native Americans, whose homeland was being usurped. Many had ongoing wars with the cattlemen who came through. All struggled to survive the fierce climate. Today, although the area now contains great cities and thriving, diversified industry and agriculture, the people are still strong and their cooking inventive. Take this highly unusual (and excellent) marmalade:

    6 pounds ripe tomatoes, skinned
        and coarsely chopped
    2 oranges
    2 lemons
    4 sticks cinnamon
    1 teaspoon whole cloves
    9 cups sugar

First, read the jelly-making hints that begin on page 194.

Put the prepared tomatoes in a colander over a bowl to allow their excess juice to drain off. Finely chop the entire oranges and lemons, skin and all (or run them in chunks in a food processor). Combine all the ingredients in a large saucepan and stir over medium-high heat until the mixture reaches a temperature of 220° F or sheets off a spoon. Fish out the cinnamon sticks and cloves and pack the marmalade into freshly sterilized jars. Process in a hot water bath. • *MAKES enough for about 9 8-ounce jars.*

Hot and Sweet Country Mustard

With so many excellent mustards on the market, why make your own? Well, mainly because you can't, as far as I know, buy one like this, and it's so very good. Mustards like this have been made in the Midwest as long as there have been kitchens there.

    ½ cup dry mustard
    ½ cup flour
    ½ cup sugar
    Pinch of salt
    ¼ cup cider vinegar

Combine the dry mustard, flour, sugar and salt, then slowly stir in the cider vinegar. Don't taste it now, because it will be horrible, but in 3 or 4 days it will have mellowed and become superb. Keeps indefinitely in a cool place. • *MAKES a bit less than 1 cup.*

Aunt Kate's Illinois Chili Sauce

Katherine Eastman Ellis, my Aunt Kate, made this great sauce for years in her Illinois kitchen, and gave my own household many sparkling jars of it.

I'm delighted to have her recipe for it, but the way she wrote it down needs a little translation for today's cooks, since it calls for such things as a peck of tomatoes and one "hot finger pepper, seeds and all." If you look up "peck," you'll find it means eight quarts, but how do you measure whole tomatoes by the quart? Also, what is a "hot finger pepper?" A jalapeño, perhaps?

I've compromised and taken a few liberties, but the chili sauce tastes just like Aunt Kate's.

12 medium-size ripe tomatoes
1 clove garlic, peeled
3 medium-size onions
2 sweet red peppers
1 tablespoon jalapeño sauce or 1
    teaspoon Louisiana hot sauce
1 cup white vinegar
½ cup sugar
1½ tablespoons salt
½ teaspoon cinnamon
½ teaspoon allspice
½ teaspoon celery seed
½ teaspoon mustard seed

Peel the tomatoes after loosening their skins by dipping them briefly in boiling water, then into cold. Core and chop them, not too coarsely. Add the garlic. Cook over moderate heat for 30 minutes. Now Aunt Kate said to remove 2 cups of the liquid that has accumulated. I've done it her way, but then put the juice back in because it seemed like such a waste. (If you don't take the excess juice out, you will have to increase the cooking time. What you want is a fairly thick sauce.)

Take the garlic out and mash it. Run the onions and red peppers through a meat grinder or food processor and add them, along with the mashed garlic, jalapeño sauce, vinegar and sugar to the tomatoes. Cook at a slow boil for 1 hour, or until the sauce reaches the thickness you wish.

Put into freshly sterilized jars (see page 194) and process in a hot water bath. • *FILLS about 7 half-pint jars.*

Heartland Bread-and-Butter Pickles

Even if you've never had any desire to make pickles, I urge you to try these masterpieces. They're simple and quick to make, and nothing you can buy in a grocery store even comes close in flavor or texture.

Because their skins haven't been waxed and they have fewer and smaller seeds, it's ideal to use pickling cucumbers (especially those called "Kirby"), available in markets and farm stands in late summer.

The usual pickling spice is made up of such savory spices as whole allspice, cloves and coriander plus bits of cinna-

mon stick and bay leaf. There will often be small hot red peppers, too; remove these little demons before making your pickles.

4 pounds pickling cucumbers (about 10 fat ones).
2 tablespoons mustard seed
1 tablespoon pickling spice (see above)
1 teaspoon celery seed
1¼ cups water
2 cups cider vinegar
2½ cups sugar
2 teaspoons salt
½ teaspoon turmeric

Slice the cucumbers as thinly as possible. (The thinnest slicing disk of a food processor is a rather large help in this task.)

Put the mustard seed, pickling spice and celery seed into a square made from a dou-ble thickness of cheesecloth; bring the cloth up into a purse shape and tie the top with a string. (Or use one of the metal balls designed to hold tea leaves.)

Combine the water, cider vinegar, sugar, salt and turmeric and the bag or ball of spices in a good-size kettle. Bring to a boil, stirring to dissolve the sugar, and boil for 2 or 3 minutes.

Now add the cucumbers and bring the liquid back to a boil. (Don't worry if at first the amount of liquid seems too small; enough will exude from the cucumber slices to cover them amply.)

After 2 minutes (watch the clock closely) remove the pot from the stove. Fill your prepared glasses with the cucumber slices and top with the liquid. Seal (see page 194). • *MAKES 8 8-ounce glasses.*

Apple Butter

The Midwest owes a man named John Chapman a tremendous debt. This visionary, known to all as Johnny Appleseed, roamed through the area, particularly Indiana, Illinois and Ohio, in the early 1800s, dressed in a coffee sack and barefoot most of the time. A vegetarian, Johnny Appleseed's mission was to bring the settlers a reliable source of fruit. He planted apple seeds wherever he went—and then returned in later years to take care of the resulting trees.

Before long, Johnny's trees were flourishing and producing such large crops of apples that ways were needed to use them up. One of the best of these ways was Apple Butter. Making this spread was a family event, since many hands were needed to stir the butter constantly for hours to prevent it from scorching. As the butter thickened, it began to spit and to get all over everything within reach. For this reason, Apple Butter making was usually done outdoors. Today, though, the butter is generally made in the oven, a major laborsaving move.

4 pounds apples, peeled, cored and sliced
1 cup water
1 cup sharp apple cider or cider vinegar
1 cup sugar or honey
1 teaspoon cinnamon
1 teaspoon ground cloves
1 teaspoon ground allspice

Cook the apples in the water and cider or cider vinegar until very soft, then add the rest of the ingredients and put in a large, fairly shallow pan in a 350° F oven. Bake, stirring every 20 minutes, for about 3 hours, or until thick.

Pack in freshly sterilized jars (see page 194) and process in a hot water bath. • *MAKES about 6 8-ounce jars. (By fruit butter standards, this is a small batch, but the recipe can be doubled or tripled.)*

Confetti Corn Relish

It's hard to find any corn relish at all in stores, let alone one as beautiful both to look at and taste as this one. Some people add shredded cabbage to their corn relish, but this seems to me to muddy the looks and the flavor. I prefer this version of an old Wisconsin recipe, which is similar to the corn relishes we took along to go with the ham that was served on most of our picnics in Iowa. The prepared mustard it contains is its real secret.

One of our favorite picnic spots was Crapo (pronounced CRAY-po) Park, which was perched on a bluff overlooking the Mississippi near Burlington. When my Aunt Camilla, who by then lived in California, flew in to Burlington to go to Mount Pleasant for the first time, the car route lay past Crapo Park. When she saw the sign, she made us turn the car around so she could take a picture of it. "My friends will never believe it otherwise," she said.

But my own favorite picnic spot was about twenty minutes from Mount Pleasant, near the town of New London. It was a grassy spot in the middle of some woods, and very pretty, but the reason I loved it was that the ground was practically cobbled with geodes. I learned how to recognize them and that if you threw them hard enough against a bigger rock, they would crack open, revealing what looked like a lining of diamonds.

I didn't think anything could be more exciting. I gathered so many of them that eventually my grandmother used them to line a goldfish pond. What a sight—dozens and dozens of sparkling little grottos! How I wish I had some of those geodes now. But at any rate, I can still make the corn relish and all the rest of the picnic feast foods and remember those lovely, leisurely days.

12 ears corn, cooked
4 large stalks celery, finely chopped
2 large onions, finely chopped
1 large green pepper, finely chopped
1 large sweet red pepper, finely chopped
1½ cups light or dark brown sugar
1½ cups cider or white vinegar
½ cup prepared (bought, that is) yellow mustard
1 teaspoon dry mustard
1 tablespoon flour
2 tablespoons salt

Cut the kernels from the ears of corn and put into a large pot with all the other ingredients. (Save the corncobs to make Corncob Jelly or Corncob Syrup.) Bring to a boil, stirring, then turn the heat down and simmer for about 30 minutes, stirring every 5 minutes. Pour into freshly sterilized jars and process in a hot water bath (see page 194). • MAKES about 4 pints.

A Taste of the Midwest— by Mail Order

People all over the country have been eating Midwestern food for years, whether they realize it or not. Take a look around your pantry shelves, plus your refrigerator and freezer and you'll see what I mean. For example:

Procter & Gamble (including Duncan Hines, etc.)—Ohio

Pillsbury (including Green Giant)—Minnesota

Smucker's (jams, peanut butter, etc.)—Ohio

Quaker Oats—Illinois

Armour (bacon, etc.)—Nebraska

Kellogg's—Michigan

Stokely (frozen vegetables, etc.)—Wisconsin

—and such shockers as:

Old El Paso Mexican foods—Missouri

Kikkoman (soy sauce, etc.)—Wisconsin

Most of the products made by these companies are very good, but better yet are the fine foods turned out by a number of small heartland companies. I've been acquainted with some of these remarkable foods for most of my life—Maytag blue cheese and Amana hams, for instance. A few, such as Wolferman's amazing English muffins, are exciting new discoveries.

All these foods are available by mail order—an easy way to bring the beautiful tastes of the Midwest into your own kitchen, wherever you live. A phone call or written request will get you catalogs and other ordering information. You'll find that many of the companies carry products other than their own food specialties. Wolferman's, for example, will be happy to sell you a toaster.

Maytag Dairy Farms
(Blue cheese is their beloved old standby, but they also now have a sharp white Cheddar, Swiss and Edam as well as cheese spreads)
P. O. Box 806
Newton, IA 50208
(800) 247-2458 or inside Iowa:
  (800) 258-2437

Omaha Steaks International
(Corn-fed beef)
4400 S. 96th St.
Omaha, NE 68103
(800) 228-9055

Wolferman's Good Things to Eat
(English muffins—two inches high and in fifteen, at last count, different flavors)
P. O. Box 15913
Lenexa, KS 66215-5913
(800) 999-0169

Amana Meat Shop & Smokehouse
(Country ham, bacon, etc.)
Amana, IA 52203
(800) 373-6328

Burgers' Smokehouse
(Hickory-smoked, sugar-cured meats)
California, MO 65018
(800) 796-4111

Strickler's Sausage Kitchen
(Beef sausage, smoked turkey, etc.)
New Glarus Foods
New Glarus, WI 53574
(800) 356-6685

Cavanaugh Lakeview Farms, Ltd.
(A miscellany of meats, including buffalo burgers and venison, and poultry, including quail—fresh, smoked and/or cooked)
P. O. Box 580
Chelsea, MI 48118
(800) 243-4438

American Spoon Foods
(Fruit preserves and butters, black walnuts, dried cherries, etc.)
P. O. Box 566
Petoskey, MI 49770
(800) 222-5886

Wicker's Barbecue Products Co.
(Missouri-style barbecue sauces, marinades and bastes)
P. O. Box 126
Hornersville, MO 63955
(800) 847-0032

Empress Chili
(Cincinnati Chili in cans)
10592 Taconic Terrace
Cincinnati, OH 45215
(513) 771-1441

Index

3

About the Author

Glenn Andrews was born in Chicago, Illinois, but has lived most of her life on the East Coast. Her love for the Midwest comes from the many summers she spent as a child with her grandparents in Mount Pleasant, Iowa. She graduated from Sarah Lawrence College, and worked for some years in an editorial capacity at Time, Inc., McGraw-Hill, and *Seventeen* magazine before turning to freelance writing. She is the author of *Impromptu Cooking* and *Mood Food* and co-author with Donald Sobel of *Encyclopedia Brown Takes the Cake*. Glenn Andrews makes her home in Williamstown, Massachusetts.